ISBN 978-0-9763065-6-6 (paperback)

Book Cover and Inside Art by Cyphur + Art & Design

To the my forever little ones

You are the source of my unwavering determination and the driving force behind every endeavor. Your boundless curiosity, resilience, and unwavering support have inspired me throughout this journey. As you grow, may this book serve as a reminder that with determination, focus, and the pursuit of your own "why," you can overcome any distractions and achieve your dreams. Always reach for the stars, my loves.

Pops

CLARITY

JONES

What's Inside ...

CLARITY

JONES

Introduction

The ability to maintain unwavering focus on your strategic goals can be the difference between success and failure. Distractions, in their various forms, stand as formidable adversaries to the ambitious entrepreneur, capable of diverting precious time and energy away from the pursuit of one's "why" – the fundamental reason driving them towards their entrepreneurial journey.

This book, "Focus, Man: Overcoming Distractions for Entrepreneurial Success," is a comprehensive guide that delves into the intricate relationship between distractions and strategic goals in the context of entrepreneurship. We'll explore the ways in which distractions infiltrate our lives, hinder our progress, and ultimately impede the realization of our entrepreneurial dreams. More importantly, we'll equip you with practical techniques and strategies, applicable at all stages of your entrepreneurial journey, to effectively combat distractions and stay aligned with your "why."

The Importance of Focus in Entrepreneurship

For entrepreneurs, focus is the compass that guides them through the often turbulent seas of business. It's the unwavering belief in their mission, the relentless pursuit of their goals, and the ability to navigate through distractions that sets them apart. In today's fast-paced and digitally connected world, maintaining that focus has become a Herculean task.

The Impact of Distractions on Strategic Goals

Distractions, both subtle and overt, can infiltrate every facet of an entrepreneur's life, from their daily routines to their long-term strategic planning. Social media notifications beckon, email inboxes overflow, and the siren song of instant gratification tempts even the most disciplined entrepreneur. These distractions, if left unattended, can erode productivity, stifle creativity, and hinder progress.

Setting the Stage for Success

But, fear not, for this book is not just about identifying distractions and their perils; it's about empowerment. It's about taking control of your focus and harnessing it as a force to propel you towards your entrepreneurial "why." By the time you reach the final chapter, you will have gained the tools and insights to cultivate a distraction-resistant mindset and environment, allowing you to steer your entrepreneurial ship toward the prosperous shores of success.

To embark on this journey together, we'll navigate through fifteen chapters that provide a structured approach to conquering distractions. We'll begin by understanding the nature of distractions, dissecting their psychology, and exploring the impact of the digital age on our ability to concentrate. Then, we'll delve into the importance of defining your entrepreneurial "why" and how it can serve as your North Star amidst the distractions.

We'll explore the science behind distractions and their cognitive and behavioral aspects. We'll dig deep into the world of digital distractions, unveiling the strategies that can help you regain control of your online life. You'll learn how to build a distraction-resistant environment and master the art of time management. Mindfulness and meditation will be your allies in strengthening your focus, and we'll uncover the secrets of habit-building and accountability that can shape your success.

Saying "no" gracefully and setting boundaries will become your tools to guard your focus. Self-care will be your armor against burnout, and you'll uncover the strategies to overcome it if it ever strikes. We'll also tackle the unexpected distractions and how to handle them effectively, ensuring that even in times of crisis, your focus remains unshaken.

You'll learn how to measure your progress, adjust your course, and celebrate the small wins along the way. To inspire you further, we'll share real-life success stories of entrepreneurs who triumphed over distractions and achieved their dreams.

In the epilogue, you'll have the chance to reflect on your entrepreneurial journey and embrace a distraction-resistant lifestyle as you move forward to new horizons of success.

But, this book is not just a journey through words; it's a practical guide that will provide you with actionable strategies, real-world examples, and valuable resources. At the end of each chapter, you'll find exercises and tips that you can implement immediately to strengthen your focus and reclaim your time.

So, whether you're a seasoned entrepreneur looking to enhance your focus or someone just starting on this thrilling path, "Unwavering Focus" will equip you with the knowledge, tools, and motivation to overcome distractions, fulfill your entrepreneurial aspirations, and ultimately lead you to the fulfillment of your "why."

Now, let's dive into the heart of the matter and begin our exploration of the complex world of distractions and the profound impact they have on your entrepreneurial journey.

Chapter 1

Understanding Distractions

Distractions, those subtle and not-so-subtle interruptions that pull us away from our intended tasks and goals, are a ubiquitous part of modern life. In the context of entrepreneurship, where time and focus are precious resources, understanding distractions is crucial. This chapter delves into the essence of distractions, breaking down their types, exploring their impact on our lives, and revealing the science behind their alluring grasp.

Defining Distractions

At its core, a distraction is anything that diverts our attention from what we are doing, often towards something less important or unrelated. Distractions come in various forms, from the incessant ping of a smartphone notification to the allure of social media scrolling, from chatty colleagues to a cluttered workspace. They lurk everywhere, waiting to snatch our focus and divert our energies.

Distractions can be external or internal. External distractions originate from our environment – the noisy construction outside our window, the incoming email alert, or a catchy billboard on our way to work. Internal distractions, on the other hand, emanate from within ourselves – racing thoughts, daydreams, or a nagging worry about an unfinished task.

Types of Distractions Entrepreneurs Face

Entrepreneurs, who often wear multiple hats and juggle numerous responsibilities, are particularly susceptible to a wide range of distractions. Let's dissect some of the common types they encounter:

1. Digital Distractions
In our hyper-connected world, digital distractions reign supreme. Smartphones, tablets, and laptops are ever-present, ready to deliver a barrage of emails, messages, and notifications. Social media platforms beckon with their endless streams of content, each designed to capture our attention and keep us scrolling.

2. Information Overload
The information age has bestowed us with unprecedented access to knowledge and data. While this is undeniably valuable, it also

presents a double-edged sword. Entrepreneurs often find themselves drowning in a sea of information, struggling to discern what is relevant from what is noise.

3. Workplace Distractions

The workplace itself can be a breeding ground for distractions. Colleagues stopping by for impromptu conversations, the constant hum of office chatter, and an overflowing inbox can disrupt even the most well-laid plans.

4. Procrastination

Procrastination, the act of delaying tasks, is a subtle but potent distraction. It often masquerades as a harmless respite – just a few more minutes of YouTube, or one more cup of coffee – only to leave you scrambling to meet deadlines later.

5. Multitasking

Entrepreneurs are often lauded for their ability to multitask, but this seemingly advantageous skill can also be a source of distraction. Switching between tasks can lead to decreased productivity and reduced quality of work.

6. Psychological Distractions

Internal distractions can be equally formidable. Worries about the future, regrets about the past, or a persistent negative thought can hijack your attention and sap your mental energy.

7. Physical Distractions

Even the physical environment can play a role. A cluttered workspace, uncomfortable seating, or poor lighting can all contribute to a less-than-optimal working environment.

The Science of Distraction

Distraction is not merely a nuisance; it has deep roots in psychology and neuroscience. Understanding the science behind distraction can shed light on why it is so challenging to maintain focus.

The Brain's Reward System

One key player in the distraction game is our brain's reward system. When we encounter something novel or pleasurable – be it a new email, a social media like, or even a snack – our brain releases dopamine, a neurotransmitter associated with pleasure and motivation. This surge of dopamine creates a rewarding feeling, making us more likely to seek out similar stimuli in the future.

In the context of distractions, this reward system can be hijacked. When our brain associates checking our email or social media with a pleasurable dopamine hit, we become more prone to interrupting our work to seek out these distractions, even if they are not essential or productive.

Attentional Bias

Another intriguing aspect of distraction is our attentional bias. This bias makes us more likely to pay attention to stimuli that are emotionally charged, personally relevant, or novel. When a distracting email from a client or an exciting news headline pops up, our attentional bias compels us to shift our focus away from our current task and toward the new and engaging information.

Task Switching and Cognitive Load

Multitasking, a common response to distractions, may seem like an efficient use of time, but it comes at a cost. Every time we switch tasks, our brain incurs a cognitive load, a mental cost associated with shifting our attention and reorienting ourselves to the new task. This cognitive load not only slows us down but can also lead to errors and decreased overall productivity.

Habituation

As we encounter the same distractions repeatedly, our brain can become habituated to them. This means that the initial rush of dopamine we experience when checking our email or social media diminishes over time. As a result, we may seek out more and more distractions in a futile attempt to recapture that initial pleasure, perpetuating a cycle of distraction and decreased productivity.

Understanding the science behind distraction equips us with valuable insights into why we succumb to distractions and why they can be so difficult to resist. Armed with this knowledge, we can begin to develop effective strategies for mitigating distractions and regaining control over our focus.

In the following chapters, we will explore practical techniques to address the various types of distractions entrepreneurs face. We will delve into the psychology of distractions, examine the impact of the digital age, and equip you with the tools to build a distraction-resistant mindset and environment. Your journey to unwavering focus and entrepreneurial success begins here.

Chapter 2

The Entrepreneur's "Why"

Amid the hustle and bustle of business endeavors, there exists a potent guiding force that fuels the aspirations and actions of every successful entrepreneur—their "why." It's the profound reason behind their entrepreneurial journey, the bedrock upon which they build their businesses, and the beacon that leads them through the challenging terrain of entrepreneurship. In this chapter, we'll delve deep into the concept of the "why," exploring its significance, uncovering its power, and revealing how it can serve as a steadfast compass to navigate the complexities of entrepreneurial life while fending off distractions.

Discovering Your Purpose

At the core of every entrepreneurial venture lies a purpose—a driving force that propels individuals to embark on this demanding journey. For some, it's a passion that ignites their soul, a mission to create something meaningful, or an unyielding desire to solve a problem they're deeply passionate about. For others, it's the pursuit of financial independence, the desire to leave a lasting legacy, or a relentless quest for personal growth and fulfillment.

The "why" is the lighthouse that helps entrepreneurs chart their course, ensuring they stay true to their core values and objectives. It's not merely about making a profit; it's about making a difference. Your "why" isn't a shallow slogan or a catchy marketing phrase; it's the profound, intrinsic motivation that drives you to endure the inevitable challenges and distractions that accompany entrepreneurship.

The Power of a Clear Vision

Your entrepreneurial "why" isn't a static concept; it's a dynamic, evolving force that propels you forward. It's the vision that you hold for yourself, your business, and the impact you intend to make on the world. A clear and compelling vision is the linchpin of your entrepreneurial journey—it's what keeps you focused when distractions beckon and adversity strikes.

A well-defined vision offers several key benefits:

1. Focus Amidst Distractions

When your vision is crystal clear, it becomes a powerful anchor that keeps you rooted in your purpose. Distractions may tug at your attention, but your unwavering commitment to your vision helps you resist the allure of short-term diversions.

2. Motivation to Persist

Entrepreneurship is fraught with challenges and setbacks. Your "why" acts as a reservoir of motivation during tough times. It reminds you of the bigger picture and why you embarked on this journey in the first place.

3. Alignment of Efforts

A clear "why" serves as a unifying force for your team. When everyone understands and believes in the same purpose, it becomes easier to align efforts and work together towards common goals, reducing internal distractions and conflicts.

4. Decision-Making Compass

Your "why" becomes a compass for decision-making. When faced with choices and distractions, you can evaluate them against your overarching purpose, making it easier to discern what aligns with your vision and what does not.

5. Resilience in the Face of Failure

Failures and setbacks are inevitable in entrepreneurship. However, a strong "why" provides the resilience needed to bounce back. It reminds you that temporary setbacks do not define your journey's ultimate trajectory.

How Your "Why" Drives Strategic Goals

Your entrepreneurial "why" is not a standalone concept; it intricately intertwines with your strategic goals. Your goals are the tangible manifestations of your "why," the stepping stones that lead you toward your vision. They provide a clear path to turn your purpose into reality.

Setting Purpose-Driven Goals

While setting strategic goals, it's crucial to ensure they are aligned with your "why." When your goals are driven by your purpose, they are more likely to inspire and motivate you. They become a source of focus, a driving force that propels you forward even when distractions lurk around every corner.

Maintaining Consistency

Consistency is the key to achieving long-term success in entrepreneurship. Your "why" acts as a touchstone that ensures you stay consistent in your actions and decisions. It prevents you from veering off course when faced with temptations or distractions that may momentarily pull you away from your goals.

Measuring Progress

Your "why" also plays a pivotal role in measuring your progress. It helps you establish key performance indicators (KPIs) that align with your overarching purpose. These KPIs become metrics of success, allowing you to track your journey and make data-driven decisions that keep distractions at bay.

Adapting to Change

In the ever-evolving landscape of entrepreneurship, adaptability is essential. Your "why" provides the guiding principles that help you navigate change. It serves as a constant amidst the turbulence, allowing you to adjust your strategies and goals while staying true to your core purpose.

Unleashing the Power of Your "Why"

Unveiling your "why" is not a one-time exercise; it's an ongoing journey of self-discovery and introspection. Here's a step-by-step guide to help you unlock the full potential of your "why":

1. Reflect on Your Passions

Begin by exploring your passions and interests. What activities or causes ignite your enthusiasm? What problems do you find yourself eager to solve? Your "why" often aligns closely with your passions.

2. Identify Your Core Values

Consider your core values—the principles that guide your life and decision-making. What matters most to you? Identifying your values can provide insight into the type of impact you want to make through entrepreneurship.

3. Define Your Vision

Craft a vivid and inspiring vision for your entrepreneurial journey. Envision the future you want to create, both for yourself and for others. This vision should encapsulate your "why" and serve as a constant reminder of your purpose.

4. Connect with Your Emotions

Your "why" is often deeply rooted in your emotions. Reflect on what moves you, what makes you feel fulfilled, and what brings you joy. These emotional connections can lead you to your purpose.

5. Seek Feedback and Input

Engage in conversations with mentors, colleagues, and friends. They may offer valuable perspectives and insights that can help you clarify your "why." Sometimes, others can see your strengths and passions more clearly than you can.

6. Test Your Purpose

As you uncover your "why," test it against your daily actions and decisions. Does it align with your current choices? Does it inspire you to stay focused and resilient in the face of distractions? If not, refine and adjust your purpose accordingly.

7. Write It Down

Once you've identified your "why," write it down. Creating a succinct and powerful statement that encapsulates your purpose can serve as a constant reminder and source of motivation.

Your entrepreneurial "why" is not a static concept but a dynamic force that evolves and deepens as you progress on your journey. Embrace this evolution, and allow your "why" to continue guiding your actions, goals, and decisions as you navigate the challenging terrain of entrepreneurship.

In the subsequent chapters, we will explore how you can harness the power of your "why" to maintain focus, overcome distractions, and steadily progress toward your entrepreneurial goals. Your purpose-driven journey to success starts with the clarity of your "why."

Chapter 3

The Psychology of Distractions

Distractions, though seemingly innocuous, possess a profound influence on our lives, particularly in the context of entrepreneurship. To effectively combat distractions, it's essential to unravel the intricate web of the human psyche that makes us susceptible to these interruptions. In this chapter, we'll delve into the psychology of distractions, exploring the cognitive biases, behavioral patterns, and psychological mechanisms that underlie our susceptibility to diversions. By gaining insight into how distractions affect our minds, we can develop strategies to safeguard our focus and advance our entrepreneurial pursuits.

Cognitive Biases and Distractions

Cognitive biases are inherent patterns of thought and perception that can skew our judgment and decision-making processes. They play a significant role in making us susceptible to distractions. Let's examine some common cognitive biases and their implications for our susceptibility to distractions:

Confirmation Bias

Confirmation bias is the tendency to seek out information that confirms our existing beliefs or opinions while ignoring or discounting contradictory evidence. In the context of distractions, confirmation bias can lead us to selectively engage with distractions that align with our preconceived notions or interests. For example, if we have a confirmation bias towards a particular social media platform, we may be more likely to engage with content from that platform while neglecting others.

Information Overload

The availability of vast amounts of information in the digital age can overwhelm our cognitive faculties. This phenomenon, known as information overload, can lead to a form of cognitive distraction. When faced with an abundance of information, we may struggle to focus on a single task, continually shifting our attention in an attempt to process it all.

Anchoring Bias

Anchoring bias occurs when we rely too heavily on the first piece of information we encounter (the "anchor") when making decisions. In the context of distractions, this bias can lead us astray. For example, if the first email we read in the morning is not urgent, but it captures our attention, it can anchor our focus on less critical tasks while more important ones remain undone.

The Fear of Missing Out (FOMO)

FOMO is a pervasive psychological phenomenon driven by the fear of missing out on something interesting or exciting happening elsewhere. In the digital age, FOMO is often associated with the constant stream of social media updates and notifications. The fear of missing out on a trending topic or a social event can lead us to frequently check our devices, interrupting our work and draining our focus.

Behavioral Patterns that Lead to Distractions

Understanding the cognitive biases that make us susceptible to distractions is just one part of the puzzle. We must also examine the behavioral patterns and habits that reinforce our distractibility:

Task Switching

The habit of frequently switching between tasks is a common behavioral pattern that fosters distraction. Task switching incurs a cognitive cost, as our brains must readjust each time we shift our focus. This not only slows us down but also diminishes the quality of our work. Entrepreneurs often fall into the trap of task switching, believing it allows them to multitask effectively when, in reality, it hinders productivity.

The Zeigarnik Effect

The Zeigarnik Effect is a psychological phenomenon that suggests we remember uncompleted or interrupted tasks more than completed ones. This can lead to a persistent preoccupation with un-finished tasks, causing us to be more prone to distractions as we attempt to address these mental "open loops."

Delayed Gratification

Delayed gratification, the ability to resist immediate rewards in favor of long-term goals, can be a powerful tool against distrac-tions. However, it's a skill that requires practice and self-discipline. Distractions often offer immediate gratification, such as the quick dopamine hit from checking social media or responding to non-ur-gent emails. Entrepreneurs must cultivate the ability to delay grat-ification to maintain focus on strategic goals.

Procrastination

Procrastination is a pervasive behavioral pattern that often results from the avoidance of tasks perceived as unpleasant or daunting. Entrepreneurs may procrastinate on important but challenging tasks, opting for easier, less important distractions instead. Over-coming procrastination is essential to mitigating distractions and advancing strategic goals.

The Dopamine Loop

The pursuit of distractions, particularly in the digital realm, trig-gers a dopamine loop. Dopamine, a neurotransmitter associated with pleasure and reward, is released when we engage with novel or enjoyable stimuli. This pleasurable sensation encourages us to seek out more distractions, perpetuating the cycle. Breaking free from the dopamine loop is crucial for regaining control over our focus.

Identifying Your Distraction Triggers

To combat distractions effectively, it's essential to identify your per-sonal distraction triggers. These triggers are the specific situations, environments, or emotional states that make you more susceptible to distractions. By recognizing your triggers, you can implement targeted strategies to mitigate their impact. Here are steps to help you identify your distraction triggers:

Self-Reflection

Take some time for self-reflection and consider the situations in which you tend to become distracted. Are there specific times of day or locations where distractions are more prevalent? Are certain emotional states, such as stress or boredom, linked to increased distractibility?

Data Analysis

Analyze your past behaviors and work patterns. Review your daily routines and work habits to pinpoint instances where distractions have disrupted your productivity. Look for patterns or recurring themes that may reveal your distraction triggers.

Self-Monitoring

Engage in self-monitoring by tracking your distractions for a period of time. Use a journal or digital tools to record instances when you become distracted and the circumstances surrounding those distractions. This observational data can provide valuable insights into your distraction triggers.

Seeking Feedback

Seek input from colleagues, friends, or family members who may have observed your distractibility patterns. They may offer an external perspective that highlights situations or behaviors you may not have noticed.

Experimentation

Experiment with strategies to mitigate distractions in situations where you suspect triggers may be at play. Try different approaches to address distractions and assess their effectiveness in maintaining your focus.

Once you've identified your distraction triggers, you can tailor your distraction-avoidance strategies to address them proactively. By understanding the cognitive biases and behavioral patterns that make you susceptible to distractions and pinpointing your specific triggers, you can take concrete steps to fortify your focus and progress toward your entrepreneurial goals. In the chapters that follow, we'll explore practical techniques to help you do just that, allowing you to navigate the distractions of entrepreneurship with resilience and determination.

Chapter 4

The Digital Age:
A Distraction Paradise

Where technology seamlessly integrates into every facet of our lives, distractions have found a fertile breeding ground. The pervasive presence of smartphones, tablets, and computers has ushered in an era where information, entertainment, and communication are just a tap or click away. While these technological marvels have undoubtedly transformed the way we work and connect, they have also created an environment ripe for distractions that can significantly impede our productivity and focus. In this chapter, we'll explore the digital landscape, uncover the various forms of digital distractions, examine their impact on our lives, and equip you with strategies to regain control over your online existence while advancing your entrepreneurial ambitions.

The Role of Technology in Distractions

Technology has revolutionized our world, offering convenience, connectivity, and unprecedented access to information. It has accelerated business operations, transformed communication, and created new opportunities for entrepreneurs. However, this digital revolution has also given rise to a multitude of distractions that can disrupt our work, encroach upon our personal lives, and undermine our ability to maintain focus.

The Smartphone Dilemma

Smartphones, those ubiquitous companions that accompany us everywhere, serve as both enablers and purveyors of distractions. While they provide essential tools for communication, organization, and productivity, they are also gateways to a world of diversions. The incessant stream of notifications, social media updates, and mobile apps beckons us to divert our attention constantly.

The Allure of Social Media

Social media platforms, designed to connect us with others and facilitate information sharing, have evolved into virtual attention battlegrounds. The dopamine-driven allure of likes, comments, and shares keeps us scrolling through newsfeeds, consuming content, and engaging in digital conversations, often at the expense of our strategic goals.

The Deluge of Notifications

The digital world bombards us with a barrage of notifications, each vying for our immediate attention. Email alerts, instant messages, app notifications, and calendar reminders compete for our focus, fracturing our attention into countless micro-tasks.

Social Media, Notifications, and Productivity

Social media and notifications, two prominent features of the digital age, warrant closer examination due to their pronounced impact on our lives and work:

The Social Media Paradox

Social media platforms, while designed to facilitate connection and information sharing, often foster an ironic sense of isolation and distractibility. The constant comparison with curated online personas, the pressure to maintain a digital presence, and the temptation to engage in endless scrolling can divert our focus and diminish our productivity.

The Notification Onslaught

Notifications, intended to keep us informed and organized, often have the opposite effect. The habit of checking notifications disrupts our workflow, interrupts deep concentration, and contributes to a state of constant partial attention. We become reactive, responding to external stimuli rather than proactively managing our priorities.

Digital Detox Strategies

To regain control over your digital life and mitigate the distractions spawned by the digital age, consider implementing the following strategies:

1. Notification Management
Take charge of your notifications. Review and customize your device and app settings to minimize interruptions. Disable non-essen-

tial notifications and opt for scheduled notification-checking times instead of responding immediately.

2. App and Social Media Usage

Set limits on your app and social media usage. Many smartphones offer features that track your screen time and app usage. Use this data to assess where your time goes and make conscious choices to reduce unnecessary digital interactions.

3. Digital Sabbaticals

Periodically disconnect from the digital world to recharge and re-focus. Designate specific times, days, or weekends for digital sab-baticals where you abstain from emails, social media, and digital devices. Use this time for reflection, relaxation, and pursuing of-fline interests.

4. Mindful Consumption

Practice mindful consumption of digital content. Before clicking on a link or engaging in digital activities, ask yourself whether it aligns with your strategic goals or serves as a genuine source of information or entertainment. Avoid mindless scrolling and aim for purposeful engagement.

5. Digital Workspace

Designate a distraction-free digital workspace. Create a separate environment for work-related digital activities, free from the temp-tations of personal apps and social media. This space serves as a sanctuary for focused work.

6. Time Blocking

Implement time blocking to structure your digital interactions. Al-locate specific time slots in your schedule for checking emails, social media, and other digital tasks. Outside these slots, resist the urge to engage with distractions.

7. Digital Minimalism

Embrace the philosophy of digital minimalism. Simplify your dig-ital toolbox, keeping only the apps and tools that serve a clear pur-pose in advancing your entrepreneurial goals. Eliminate redundant or rarely used applications.

8. Unplugged Mornings and Evenings
Begin and end your days without digital distractions. Establish an unplugged morning routine that prioritizes activities such as meditation, exercise, or reading before diving into digital interactions. Likewise, unwind in the evening without the interference of screens to promote restful sleep.

Balancing Technology and Focus

While the digital age has introduced distractions into our lives, it also offers a wealth of tools and resources to enhance productivity and entrepreneurship. The key is to strike a balance between leveraging technology's benefits and mitigating its distractions.

Leveraging Digital Productivity Tools

Explore digital tools designed to boost productivity. Project management apps, communication platforms, and time-tracking software can help you stay organized and efficient. Utilize productivity apps to streamline your tasks and maintain focus.

Digital Well-Being

Many devices now offer digital well-being features that allow you to monitor your digital habits. Use these tools to gain insights into your usage patterns and make informed decisions about managing distractions.

The Power of Intention

Approach your digital interactions with intentionality. Before engaging with digital content or devices, remind yourself of your strategic goals and purpose. This conscious awareness can help you resist distractions and maintain focus.

Continuous Adaptation

The digital landscape is constantly evolving, with new distractions emerging regularly. Stay vigilant and adapt your strategies as needed. Regularly assess the effectiveness of your digital detox efforts and make adjustments accordingly.

Accountability and Support

Engage in mutual accountability with colleagues, friends, or mentors to support each other in managing digital distractions. Share your goals, progress, and challenges, and hold each other accountable for maintaining focus.

The digital age, with its myriad distractions, poses both challenges and opportunities for entrepreneurs. While the allure of technology can divert our focus, it also equips us with tools and resources to thrive in a fast-paced business environment. By understanding the digital landscape, recognizing the impact of social media and notifications, and implementing digital detox strategies, you can regain control over your online existence, fortify your focus, and harness the power of technology to advance your entrepreneurial goals. In the subsequent chapters, we will delve further into techniques and practices to strengthen your ability to maintain focus and navigate the distractions of entrepreneurship with resilience and determination.

Chapter 5

Creating a Distraction Resistant Environment

In the pursuit of unwavering focus and entrepreneurial success, it's not enough to solely rely on personal discipline and willpower to combat distractions. Creating a distraction-resistant environment is equally crucial. Your physical surroundings, workspaces, and daily routines play a pivotal role in shaping your ability to stay on course and fend off interruptions. In this chapter, we will explore the importance of crafting a distraction-resistant environment, offering practical insights and strategies to fortify your surroundings and optimize your workspaces for maximum focus and productivity.

The Significance of Your Environment

Your environment exerts a powerful influence on your behavior, habits, and focus. The principle of environmental psychology underscores the dynamic relationship between individuals and their surroundings. By intentionally shaping your environment to align with your goals and minimize distractions, you can bolster your capacity to stay on track and maintain your strategic objectives.

Minimizing Decision Fatigue

Entrepreneurs often face an abundance of decisions each day, from business strategy choices to operational details. Decision fatigue can set in when too many choices deplete your cognitive resources. A distraction-resistant environment reduces decision fatigue by eliminating unnecessary options and streamlining your surroundings.

Enhancing Self-Control

Willpower and self-control are finite resources that can be depleted over the course of a day. Your environment can act as a buffer, reducing the need for constant self-control in the face of distractions. By proactively designing your workspace, you can minimize the need for willpower to resist temptations.

Fostering Productive Habits

Habits are formed through repetition and consistency. Your environment plays a vital role in reinforcing these habits. A distraction-resistant environment encourages productive behaviors by making it easier to engage in focused work and minimizing the triggers of distraction.

The Elements of a Distraction Resistant Environment

To create a distraction-resistant environment, consider the following elements and strategies:

1. Workspace Design
Designate a specific area for focused work within your workspace. Ensure that this area is comfortable, well-lit, and free from unnecessary clutter. Consider ergonomic furniture and tools to enhance your physical comfort during extended work sessions.

2. Declutter and Organize
Clutter in your workspace can be a significant source of distraction. Regularly declutter your workspace by removing items that are not essential to your work. Keep only the tools and materials you use regularly, and organize them for easy access.

3. Minimize Visual Distractions
Opt for a workspace with minimal visual distractions. If possible, position your desk or workspace away from high-traffic areas or distracting views. Use curtains, blinds, or screens to control natural light and reduce visual distractions.

4. Noise Control
Noise can be a major distraction, but you can mitigate its impact. Invest in noise-canceling headphones or white noise machines to create a more serene work environment. Alternatively, consider playing instrumental or ambient music if it helps you concentrate.

5. Digital Boundaries
Set boundaries for digital devices and online activities within your

workspace. Create a separate digital-free zone where you conduct focused work. When you enter this zone, it signals your brain that it's time to concentrate.

6. Ergonomics
Prioritize ergonomics to support comfort and productivity. Choose an ergonomic chair and desk setup that promotes good posture and reduces physical discomfort. An uncomfortable workspace can lead to frequent breaks and distractions.

7. Personalize Your Space
Personalize your workspace with items that motivate and inspire you. This could include motivational quotes, artwork, or plants. A personalized environment can create a positive atmosphere and boost your mood, helping you stay focused.

8. Time Management Tools
Integrate time management tools into your environment. Use visible calendars, to-do lists, or task boards to keep track of your priorities and deadlines. When these tools are easily accessible, you're less likely to forget or overlook essential tasks.

9. Create a Routine
Establish a daily routine that includes designated work hours and breaks. A structured routine not only enhances your productivity but also minimizes the temptation to engage in distractions during work hours.

10. Boundaries with Others
Communicate boundaries with colleagues, family members, or housemates who share your workspace. Make it clear when you're in focused work mode and request their cooperation in minimizing disruptions.

The Power of Rituals

Rituals are intentional actions or routines that signal a specific mindset or activity. Incorporating rituals into your workday can help you transition into a focused state and minimize distractions:

The Start-of-Day Ritual

Begin your workday with a deliberate start-of-day ritual. This could involve setting an intention for the day, reviewing your goals, or engaging in a brief meditation or mindfulness practice. A start-of-day ritual signals to your brain that it's time to shift into work mode.

The Transition Ritual

Create a transition ritual that marks the shift from non-work activities to focused work. This could be as simple as changing your outfit or lighting a specific candle. The act of transitioning with intention can reduce the carryover of distractions from other parts of your day.

The End-of-Day Ritual

Conclude your workday with an end-of-day ritual that signals the end of work-related activities. This ritual might involve reviewing your accomplishments, setting tasks for the next day, or tidying your workspace. An end-of-day ritual helps you mentally detach from work and unwind.

Implementing a Distraction-Resistant Routine

Crafting a distraction-resistant environment is not a one-time task; it requires ongoing maintenance and adaptation. To implement a distraction-resistant routine, follow these steps:

1. Assessment
Begin by assessing your current workspace and routine. Identify elements that contribute to distractions and areas where improvements can be made.

2. Prioritization
Prioritize the changes that will have the most significant impact on reducing distractions. Focus on the elements that align with your specific needs and work style.

3. Gradual Implementation
Introduce changes gradually to avoid overwhelming yourself. Start with one or two adjustments, such as decluttering your workspace or establishing a start-of-day ritual.

4. Consistency
Consistency is key to establishing a distraction-resistant routine. Commit to your chosen changes and incorporate them into your daily work habits.

5. Evaluation and Adaptation
Regularly evaluate the effectiveness of your distraction-resistant environment and routine. Make adjustments as needed based on your evolving needs and experiences.

6. Accountability
Share your goals and progress with colleagues, friends, or mentors who can hold you accountable for maintaining a distraction-resistant routine. Their support can help reinforce your commitment.

By proactively shaping your environment, implementing rituals, and adhering to a structured routine, you can create a distraction-resistant oasis that empowers you to stay focused on your entrepreneurial goals. The environment you cultivate becomes an ally in your quest for productivity and success, reducing the allure of distractions and fostering an atmosphere of unwavering dedication to your strategic objectives. In the following chapters, we will explore additional techniques and strategies to further enhance your ability to maintain focus and overcome the distractions that entrepreneurship may present.

Chapter 6

Mastering Time Management

Time, the most finite and precious resource in the entrepreneurial journey, is both a friend and a foe. Effectively managing time is the cornerstone of productivity and a critical skill for any entrepreneur seeking to navigate the complex landscape of distractions and strategic goals. In this chapter, we will delve into the art and science of time management, exploring techniques, tools, and strategies to help you optimize your use of time, stay focused on your objectives, and achieve remarkable results in your entrepreneurial endeavors.

The Time Management Imperative

In the realm of entrepreneurship, where demands are constant and distractions abundant, effective time management is non-negotiable. It empowers you to:

1. Prioritize Strategic Goals

Time management allows you to allocate your most valuable resource—time—to your strategic objectives. It ensures that your efforts are aligned with your long-term vision and prevents distractions from derailing your progress.

2. Enhance Productivity

Efficient time management enables you to make the most of each working day. By optimizing your workflow and minimizing time wasted on non-essential tasks, you can accomplish more in less time.

3. Reduce Stress

Properly managing your time reduces the stress and anxiety that often accompany a chaotic schedule. It provides structure and predictability, allowing you to approach your work with a sense of control.

4. Foster Work-Life Balance

Entrepreneurship can be all-consuming, but effective time management helps you strike a balance between work and personal life. It allows you to allocate dedicated time for relaxation, family, and personal interests.

Time Management Principles

Mastering time management begins with understanding and applying fundamental principles that serve as the foundation for effective time utilization:

1. Setting Clear Goals
Define your strategic goals and objectives with utmost clarity. Your goals provide the framework for prioritizing tasks and activities. When you know what you're working towards, it becomes easier to allocate time efficiently.

2. Prioritization
Not all tasks are created equal. The Eisenhower Matrix, a time management tool, categorizes tasks into four quadrants: urgent and important, important but not urgent, urgent but not important, and neither urgent nor important. Focus your efforts on tasks in the first two quadrants, which align with your strategic goals.

3. Time Blocking
Time blocking involves allocating specific blocks of time to particular tasks or activities. By structuring your day into time blocks dedicated to different types of work, you can maintain focus and prevent interruptions.

4. The Two-Minute Rule
The two-minute rule suggests that if a task can be completed in two minutes or less, you should do it immediately. This prevents minor tasks from piling up and becoming distractions later.

5. The Pomodoro Technique
The Pomodoro Technique breaks your work into intervals, typically 25 minutes in length, followed by a short break. This structured approach can enhance focus and productivity while preventing burnout.

6. Avoiding Multitasking
Contrary to popular belief, multitasking is often counterproductive. It leads to reduced efficiency, increased errors, and decreased overall productivity. Focus on one task at a time to maximize your

effectiveness.

Tools for Time Management

Various tools and technologies can aid in your time management efforts:

1. To-Do Lists
Traditional to-do lists or digital task management apps can help you organize your daily tasks and priorities. Break larger projects into smaller, actionable tasks to make them more manageable.

2. Calendar Apps
Calendar apps allow you to schedule appointments, meetings, and time blocks for specific tasks. Sync your calendar with other devices to stay informed about your schedule.

3. Time Tracking Software
Time tracking software records how you spend your time, helping you identify areas of inefficiency. This data can inform your time management strategies.

4. Project Management Tools
Project management tools offer features for task allocation, collaboration, and progress tracking. They are valuable for managing complex projects and teams.

5. Note-Taking Apps
Capture ideas, notes, and insights in note-taking apps. Organize your thoughts and refer back to them when needed to avoid distractions caused by forgotten tasks or ideas.

Strategies for Effective Time Management

To master time management in the entrepreneurial context, consider implementing the following strategies:

1. The 80/20 Rule (Pareto Principle)
The 80/20 rule suggests that roughly 80% of your results come from 20% of your efforts. Identify the tasks and activities that yield

the most significant impact on your strategic goals and allocate more time to them.

2. Time Audit
Conduct a time audit to track how you spend your days. Analyze the data to identify areas where time is wasted or misallocated. This insight will guide your efforts to optimize your schedule.

3. Delegate and Outsource
Entrepreneurs often wear many hats, but not all tasks require your direct involvement. Delegate or outsource tasks that can be handled by others, allowing you to focus on high-priority activities.

4. Time Batching
Group similar tasks together in time blocks. For instance, dedicate a specific block of time to handle emails, another for meetings, and another for creative work. This reduces context switching and enhances focus.

5. Say No Strategically
While saying yes to opportunities is essential, saying no strategically is equally important. Evaluate new commitments in light of your strategic goals, and decline those that do not align.

6. Limit Meeting Time
Meetings can consume a substantial portion of your workday. Set clear objectives for meetings, limit their duration, and only invite necessary participants.

7. Regular Breaks
Taking short, regular breaks can refresh your mind and prevent burnout. Use techniques like the Pomodoro Technique to incorporate breaks into your workday.

8. Review and Reflect
Regularly review your goals and time management strategies. Reflect on your progress and make adjustments as needed to stay aligned with your objectives.

The Digital Detox for Time Management

Managing time effectively also involves a digital detox—a deliberate effort to minimize digital distractions and regain control over your attention. Consider these digital detox strategies:

1. Digital Sabbaticals
Designate periods for digital detox where you disconnect from emails, social media, and digital devices. Use this time for focused work, relaxation, or offline activities.

2. Notification Control
Customize your device and app notification settings to minimize interruptions. Disable non-essential notifications and establish specific times for checking messages.

3. App Usage Tracking
Use app usage tracking features on smartphones to monitor how much time you spend on different apps. This data can help you make informed decisions about app usage.

4. Email Management
Implement email management strategies, such as batching email responses and unsubscribing from non-essential newsletters. Use filters and folders to organize your inbox.

5. Screen Time Limits
Set screen time limits on your devices to prevent excessive use of digital apps and platforms. Enforce these limits to regain control over your digital habits.

Time Management as a Skill

Time management is a skill that can be cultivated and refined over time. It requires ongoing effort and a willingness to adapt to changing circumstances. As you progress in your entrepreneurial journey, the demands on your time may shift, and new distractions may arise. Therefore, it's essential to view time management as a dynamic skill that evolves with your needs.

Mastering time management is a linchpin of success for entrepreneurs seeking to achieve their strategic goals while navigating the distractions of the modern world. By embracing fundamental principles, employing effective tools and strategies, and maintaining a digital detox regimen, you can optimize your use of time, enhance productivity, and safeguard your focus. In the subsequent chapters, we will delve deeper into techniques and practices that will further empower you to overcome distractions and forge a path toward entrepreneurial triumph.

Chapter 7

Mindfulness and Meditation

In the fast-paced world of entrepreneurship, where distractions abound and the pursuit of strategic goals can be relentless, the practice of mindfulness and meditation stands as a powerful ally. These techniques, rooted in ancient wisdom and supported by modern science, offer entrepreneurs a profound way to manage distractions, enhance focus, and achieve a deeper sense of clarity and resilience. In this chapter, we will explore the principles of mindfulness and meditation, their relevance in the entrepreneurial context, and practical approaches for incorporating them into your daily routine.

The Essence of Mindfulness

At its core, mindfulness is the practice of being fully present in the moment, with non-judgmental awareness of your thoughts, emotions, and sensations. It involves paying attention to your experiences as they unfold, without getting caught up in the past or projecting into the future. Mindfulness is about embracing the present with openness and acceptance.

The Relevance of Mindfulness for Entrepreneurs

In the entrepreneurial world, mindfulness plays a crucial role in managing the manifold distractions and challenges that can hinder your progress. Here's why it's particularly relevant:

1. Distraction Management
Mindfulness equips you with the ability to recognize distractions as they arise and choose how to respond to them consciously. It helps you avoid getting entangled in the allure of diversions and maintain your focus on strategic goals.

2. Stress Reduction
Entrepreneurship often brings high levels of stress and uncertainty. Mindfulness practices have been shown to reduce stress, improve emotional regulation, and enhance resilience in the face of challenges.

3. Decision-Making Clarity

Clear decision-making is essential for entrepreneurs. Mindfulness cultivates mental clarity and objectivity, enabling you to make informed and strategic decisions rather than reacting impulsively.

4. Creativity and Innovation

Entrepreneurs rely on creativity and innovation to drive their ventures. Mindfulness can foster a mindset of curiosity and creativity, encouraging novel solutions to problems and the exploration of new opportunities.

Mindfulness Practices for Entrepreneurs

Incorporating mindfulness into your daily routine need not be complex or time-consuming. Here are several practical mindfulness practices tailored to the entrepreneurial context:

1. Mindful Breathing

Mindful breathing is a fundamental practice that involves paying close attention to your breath. Find a quiet space, sit comfortably, and focus your awareness on the sensation of your breath as it enters and leaves your nostrils or the rise and fall of your abdomen. When your mind inevitably wanders, gently bring your attention back to your breath without judgment.

This practice can be done for just a few minutes at any time during your day. It serves as a quick reset for regaining focus and reducing stress.

2. Body Scan

The body scan is a mindfulness practice that involves systematically directing your attention to different parts of your body. Start at the top of your head and slowly move your focus down to your toes, noticing any sensations, tension, or discomfort along the way. This practice promotes bodily awareness and relaxation.

A short body scan can be integrated into your breaks or as a prelude to a more extended meditation session.

3. Mindful Walking

Entrepreneurs often spend long hours seated at desks or in meetings. Mindful walking provides an opportunity to break free from sedentary routines and practice mindfulness while on the move. Choose a quiet space, walk slowly, and pay attention to the sensations in your feet as they lift, move, and touch the ground. Feel the movement of your body as you walk.

Mindful walking can be particularly effective as a transition between tasks or during breaks, allowing you to clear your mind and refresh your focus.

4. Mindful Eating

In the rush of entrepreneurship, meals are often hurried or skipped altogether. Mindful eating invites you to savor each bite and fully engage with your food. Pay attention to the colors, textures, and flavors of your meal. Chew slowly and be present with each mouthful. Practicing mindful eating not only enhances your connection with your food but also provides a brief respite from the demands of the day.

5. Mindful Listening

Effective communication is a cornerstone of entrepreneurship. Mindful listening involves giving your full attention to the speaker without formulating your response in advance or allowing distractions to interfere. Listen to the words, tone, and emotions conveyed by the speaker.

Engaging in mindful listening can improve your ability to understand others, make meaningful connections, and enhance collaboration.

6. Mindful Technology Use

As an entrepreneur, you are likely tethered to digital devices. Mindful technology use encourages you to engage with technology consciously. Before checking your email, social media, or notifications, take a moment to pause and center yourself. Be aware of your intention and the potential distractions before proceeding.

This practice can prevent impulsive digital distractions and promote intentional online interactions.

Meditation: A Deeper Dive

Meditation is a structured and intentional practice that cultivates mindfulness and other positive qualities of mind. While there are various meditation techniques, we'll explore two well-known forms that are particularly beneficial for entrepreneurs: focused attention meditation and loving-kindness meditation.

Focused Attention Meditation

Focused attention meditation involves concentrating your attention on a single object or point of focus, such as your breath, a candle flame, or a specific thought or phrase. When your mind wanders, gently guide your focus back to the chosen object. This practice enhances your ability to sustain attention and reduces the impact of distractions.

To start, find a quiet place to sit comfortably. Close your eyes and bring your awareness to your breath. Observe each inhale and exhale, counting each breath if it helps. When your mind wanders or becomes distracted, return your focus to your breath.

Loving-Kindness Meditation (Metta)

Loving-kindness meditation, often called Metta, is a practice that cultivates feelings of compassion, love, and goodwill toward oneself and others. It is particularly valuable for enhancing empathy, reducing stress, and fostering positive relationships—a valuable skill for entrepreneurs working with teams, clients, and partners.

To practice loving-kindness meditation, find a quiet space and sit comfortably. Close your eyes and bring to mind a person, including yourself, for whom you wish to send loving-kindness. Repeat phrases like "May you be happy. May you be healthy. May you be safe. May you live with ease." As you recite these phrases, visualize the person experiencing these qualities. Gradually extend this practice to other individuals, including those you may have conflicts with or find challenging.

Creating a Mindful Routine

Incorporating mindfulness and meditation into your daily routine may initially feel like an additional demand on your time. However, the benefits of enhanced focus, stress reduction, and improved decision-making are worth the investment. Here's how to create a mindful routine:

1. Start Small
Begin with short sessions of mindfulness or meditation, ranging from a few minutes to ten minutes. As you build the habit, gradually extend the duration of your practice.

2. Consistency Matters
Consistency is key to reaping the rewards of mindfulness and meditation. Schedule your practice at a specific time each day, whether it's in the morning, during breaks, or before bed.

3. Be Patient and Non-Judgmental
Mindfulness is not about achieving perfection or a particular state of mind. It's about observing your experiences without judgment. Be patient with yourself, and acknowledge that the mind naturally wanders during practice.

4. Combine Mindfulness with Daily Activities
Integrate mindfulness into your daily routines. For example, practice mindful breathing while waiting for a meeting to start or engage in a short body scan before a crucial presentation.

5. Track Your Progress
Keep a journal to document your mindfulness and meditation experiences. Reflect on any changes in your focus, stress levels, or overall well-being over time.

The Science of Mindfulness

Numerous studies have explored the effects of mindfulness and meditation on the brain and overall well-being. Research findings suggest that regular mindfulness practice can:

Enhance Attention: Mindfulness training has been shown to improve attention and focus, making it easier to resist distractions and stay on task.

Reduce Stress: Mindfulness reduces the production of stress hormones and enhances the body's ability to manage stress, leading to reduced feelings of anxiety and overwhelm.

Improve Emotional Regulation: Mindfulness practices increase awareness of emotions and improve the ability to regulate them, reducing impulsive reactions and enhancing decision-making.

Enhance Resilience: Mindfulness fosters resilience by increasing one's capacity to cope with adversity and bounce back from setbacks.

Promote Creativity: Mindfulness practices can stimulate creative thinking by encouraging a mindset of curiosity and openness to new ideas.

Mindfulness and meditation are potent tools that entrepreneurs can wield to navigate the distractions and demands of their professional journeys. By cultivating a practice of mindfulness and incorporating meditation into your daily routine, you can enhance your focus, reduce stress, and foster a deeper sense of clarity and resilience.

These practices offer not only personal benefits but also ripple effects throughout your entrepreneurial endeavors, influencing your decision-making, relationships, and capacity to innovate. As you continue your entrepreneurial path, remember that mindfulness and meditation are valuable resources to support your quest for strategic success and personal fulfillment. In the forthcoming chapters, we will explore additional techniques and strategies to bolster your ability to overcome distractions and realize your entrepreneurial vision.

Chapter 8

Building Strong Habits

Habits are the invisible architects of our lives. They shape our daily routines, influence our decisions, and ultimately define our outcomes. In the entrepreneurial landscape, where distractions are abundant, the power of habit becomes a formidable ally. Building strong habits that align with your strategic goals can help you overcome distractions, enhance focus, and consistently make progress toward your vision. In this chapter, we will delve into the science of habit formation, explore practical strategies for building and sustaining productive habits, and uncover the role of habits in the entrepreneurial journey.

The Science of Habit Formation

Habits are automatic behaviors that occur without conscious thought or effort. They are etched into the neural pathways of our brains, allowing us to perform routine actions with minimal cognitive load. Understanding the science of habit formation is essential for entrepreneurs seeking to harness this cognitive machinery for their benefit.

The Habit Loop

Habit formation follows a loop consisting of three key elements: cue, routine, and reward.

Cue: This is the trigger or signal that initiates the habit. It can be a specific time, location, emotional state, or preceding action. For example, feeling stressed (cue) might trigger the habit of reaching for a snack (routine).

Routine: The routine is the behavior or action that follows the cue. It's the habit itself, whether it's checking emails, exercising, or any other repeated action.

Reward: The reward is the positive outcome or feeling associated with the habit. It reinforces the habit loop by providing a sense of satisfaction or pleasure. In the example of snacking, the reward could be the temporary relief of stress or a pleasurable taste.

Habit Formation Process

Habit formation occurs through a process of repetition and reinforcement. When you repeatedly perform a behavior in response to a specific cue and experience a rewarding outcome, the habit loop becomes stronger. Over time, the habit becomes automatic, requiring minimal conscious effort to initiate.

The Entrepreneurial Significance of Habits

In the entrepreneurial realm, cultivating productive habits can yield substantial advantages:

Consistency: Habits provide a framework for consistency in your actions, ensuring that you make progress toward your strategic goals day in and day out.

Focus: Habitual behaviors require less cognitive effort, allowing you to maintain focus on important tasks and decisions rather than expending mental energy on routine activities.

Resilience: Strong habits help you stay on track even in the face of distractions or setbacks. They act as a reliable anchor in the tumultuous waters of entrepreneurship.

Efficiency: Habits streamline your workflow, making it easier to complete tasks efficiently and allocate your time effectively.

Strategies for Building Strong Habits

Building strong habits is a deliberate and iterative process. Whether you aim to establish habits that enhance your productivity, boost your well-being, or align with your entrepreneurial goals, the following strategies can guide you on your journey:

1. Identify Your Goals
Begin by clearly defining the strategic goals you wish to achieve. Your habits should align with these objectives and support your long-term vision.

2. Start Small
Start with small, manageable habits. Trying to implement too many changes at once can be overwhelming and unsustainable. Focus on one or two habits to begin with.

3. Choose Key Habits
Identify the habits that have the most significant impact on your goals. These are often referred to as "keystone habits" and can trigger a positive ripple effect in other areas of your life or business.

4. Establish Cue-Routine-Reward Loops
Design your habits by creating clear cue-routine-reward loops. Determine the cue that will initiate the habit, define the behavior (routine), and identify the reward that reinforces the habit.

5. Be Consistent
Consistency is paramount in habit formation. Commit to performing the habit daily, or on specific days and times, to reinforce the loop.

6. Track Your Progress
Keep a record of your habit-building journey. Use a journal or habit-tracking app to monitor your consistency and celebrate your successes.

7. Leverage Technology
Technology can aid habit formation. Set reminders, use habit-tracking apps, or incorporate habit-building features into your digital devices to stay on track.

8. Accountability
Share your habit-building goals with an accountability partner or mentor who can provide support and hold you responsible for maintaining your habits.

9. Mindfulness
Practice mindfulness to increase your awareness of your habits and their effects. Mindfulness can help you recognize and change habits that may be counterproductive or no longer serve your goals.

10. Overcome Resistance

Expect resistance when forming new habits, especially in the initial stages. Push through moments of resistance by reminding yourself of the long-term benefits and rewards.

Examples of Productive Entrepreneurial Habits

While the specific habits you cultivate should align with your unique goals and circumstances, here are examples of productive entrepreneurial habits that can be adapted to suit your needs:

1. Morning Routine

Establish a morning routine that sets a positive tone for the day. Include activities such as meditation, exercise, goal setting, and reviewing your schedule.

2. Task Prioritization

Prioritize your tasks and projects daily. Use techniques like the Eisenhower Matrix to distinguish between urgent and important tasks, ensuring that you focus on high-impact activities.

3. Time Blocking

Implement time blocking to allocate dedicated blocks of time to specific tasks or categories of work. This technique helps you maintain focus and avoid distractions.

4. Continuous Learning

Cultivate a habit of continuous learning and skill development. Dedicate time each day or week to acquiring new knowledge and staying up-to-date in your industry.

5. Networking

Commit to regular networking efforts. Whether through attending industry events, connecting on social media, or reaching out to potential collaborators, networking can open doors to opportunities.

6. Healthy Lifestyle Choices

Prioritize a healthy lifestyle by establishing habits related to nutrition, exercise, and sleep. A strong physical foundation enhances your mental and emotional resilience.

7. Reflective Practice
Incorporate a reflective practice into your routine. Review your achievements, setbacks, and lessons learned at regular intervals to inform your future decisions.

8. Goal Review
Regularly review your strategic goals and progress toward them. Adjust your habits as needed to stay aligned with your evolving vision.

9. Communication
Practice effective communication habits, both in written and verbal form. Clear and timely communication is essential in the world of entrepreneurship.

10. Delegation
Cultivate the habit of delegation. Recognize when tasks can be outsourced or assigned to others, freeing up your time for more strategic activities.

Habit Maintenance and Adaptation

Once you have successfully established a habit, the work isn't over. Habits require maintenance and occasional adaptation to remain effective. Here are some considerations for habit maintenance:

1. Review and Adjust
Regularly review your habits to ensure they remain relevant to your goals. If a habit no longer serves its intended purpose, modify it or replace it with a more suitable one.

2. Overcoming Plateaus
It's common to experience plateaus or periods of stagnation in habit building. During these times, consider tweaking your routine, increasing the challenge, or seeking inspiration from others who have successfully navigated similar plateaus.

3. Celebrate Milestones

Acknowledge and celebrate your milestones and achievements along the habit-building journey. Positive reinforcement can strengthen your commitment to your habits.

4. Adapt to Change

Be flexible in adapting your habits to changing circumstances. Life as an entrepreneur is dynamic, and your habits may need to evolve to accommodate new challenges and opportunities.

The Entrepreneurial Advantage

Entrepreneurship is a journey filled with uncertainties and distractions, but it's also a realm where deliberate habit-building can lead to remarkable success. By identifying your strategic goals, choosing key habits, and applying effective habit formation strategies, you can build a foundation of consistent, focused, and productive behaviors.

As these habits become ingrained in your daily life, you'll find that distractions lose their grip, and progress toward your entrepreneurial vision becomes more predictable and achievable. In the forthcoming chapters, we will explore additional techniques and strategies to fortify your ability to overcome distractions and propel yourself toward entrepreneurial triumph.

Chapter 9

Accountability Partners
and Networking

The journey to success can be both exhilarating and challenging. Distractions lurk at every turn, threatening to divert your focus from strategic goals. However, by enlisting the support of accountability partners and engaging in strategic networking, you can strengthen your resolve, gain valuable insights, and overcome distractions more effectively. In this chapter, we will explore the profound impact of accountability partnerships and the art of networking in the entrepreneurial context.

The Power of Accountability Partnerships

Accountability partnerships are a dynamic and mutually beneficial relationship between two individuals who share their goals, progress, and challenges with each other. These partnerships are founded on the principle of mutual support and the commitment to hold each other accountable for taking action toward their respective objectives. Let's delve into the significance of accountability partnerships in the entrepreneurial journey:

1. Enhanced Focus and Commitment
When you have an accountability partner, you're more likely to stay focused on your strategic goals. The knowledge that someone else is tracking your progress and expecting results can provide a powerful incentive to remain committed to your objectives.

2. Structured Goal Setting
Accountability partnerships often involve setting clear and specific goals. This structured approach ensures that your goals are well-defined and aligned with your strategic vision.

3. Motivation and Encouragement
Having an accountability partner means you have a source of motivation and encouragement at your side. During challenging times or when distractions loom large, your partner can offer support, guidance, and words of encouragement.

4. Feedback and Problem-Solving
Accountability partners serve as a sounding board for your ideas and a source of constructive feedback. They can help you navigate obstacles and find solutions to the challenges that arise in your en-

trepreneurial journey.

5. Shared Resources and Networks

Through your accountability partner, you gain access to their resources, networks, and expertise. This expanded reach can open doors to opportunities and collaborations that may have remained hidden otherwise.

6. Accountability to Action

The essence of an accountability partnership lies in the commitment to action. Regular check-ins and progress reports ensure that your intentions are translated into concrete steps and results.

Establishing Effective Accountability Partnerships

Creating a successful accountability partnership requires careful planning and nurturing. Here are the key steps to establish and maintain an effective accountability partnership:

1. Clarify Goals and Expectations

Before entering into an accountability partnership, clearly define your goals and expectations. What are you both looking to achieve? How often will you check in? What are the preferred communication channels? Ensure alignment from the outset.

2. Select the Right Partner

Choose your accountability partner wisely. Look for someone who shares your commitment to personal and professional growth and who brings complementary skills or knowledge to the table.

3. Set SMART Goals

SMART goals are specific, measurable, achievable, relevant, and time-bound. Both you and your partner should set SMART goals that serve as the foundation of your partnership.

4. Establish Regular Check-Ins

Determine a schedule for your check-ins. This could be weekly, bi-weekly, or monthly, depending on your preferences and the nature of your goals.

5. Honest and Constructive Feedback

Create an atmosphere of trust where honest and constructive feedback is valued. Be open to receiving feedback from your partner and provide it in return.

6. Celebrate Achievements

Celebrate your successes, no matter how small. Acknowledging and celebrating achievements reinforces the sense of progress and accomplishment.

7. Adapt and Evolve

Recognize that your goals and circumstances may change over time. Be flexible and willing to adapt your accountability partnership to meet evolving needs.

8. Maintain Communication

Consistent communication is vital to the success of your partnership. Keep the lines of communication open, even when challenges arise.

9. Hold Each Other Accountable

The heart of accountability partnerships is accountability itself. Hold each other responsible for taking action and making progress toward your goals.

Networking: The Entrepreneur's Lifeline

Networking is an integral part of the entrepreneurial journey. It involves building and nurturing relationships with individuals, organizations, and communities within your industry or area of interest. Effective networking offers a multitude of benefits for entrepreneurs facing distractions and seeking to achieve their strategic goals:

1. Access to Resources

Networking provides access to a vast pool of resources, including mentors, investors, suppliers, and potential collaborators. These resources can prove invaluable in overcoming challenges and seizing opportunities.

2. Knowledge Sharing

Through networking, you can tap into the collective knowledge and expertise of your peers. Engaging in discussions, attending industry events, and participating in forums or online communities can provide insights and solutions to help you navigate distractions.

3. Collaborative Opportunities

Entrepreneurial success often involves collaborations and partnerships. Networking can lead to opportunities to collaborate on projects, share resources, or jointly tackle industry challenges.

4. Market Insights

Staying connected with your industry or niche through networking allows you to gain insights into market trends, customer preferences, and emerging opportunities. This knowledge is vital for making informed strategic decisions.

5. Personal Growth

Networking fosters personal growth by exposing you to diverse perspectives, ideas, and experiences. It can broaden your horizons, challenge your assumptions, and stimulate your creativity.

6. Mentorship and Guidance

Establishing connections with experienced individuals in your field can lead to mentorship opportunities. A mentor can provide guidance, share their experiences, and offer valuable advice on navigating distractions and achieving your strategic goals.

7. Visibility and Credibility

Networking enhances your visibility within your industry or community. Building a strong reputation and establishing credibility can attract opportunities and partnerships.

8. Emotional Support

Entrepreneurship can be a rollercoaster of emotions. Networking provides a support system of like-minded individuals who understand the unique challenges and triumphs of the entrepreneurial journey.

Strategies for Effective Networking

Effective networking goes beyond collecting business cards or making superficial connections. It requires intention, strategy, and a genuine commitment to building meaningful relationships. Here are strategies for effective networking in the entrepreneurial world:

1. Identify Your Networking Goals

Begin by clarifying your networking goals. What do you hope to achieve through networking? Whether it's finding potential collaborators, investors, or mentors, having clear objectives will guide your networking efforts.

2. Choose the Right Events and Platforms

Select networking events, conferences, or online platforms that align with your goals and target audience. Quality trumps quantity when it comes to networking opportunities.

3. Prepare Your Elevator Pitch

Craft a concise and compelling elevator pitch that succinctly describes who you are, what you do, and what you're seeking. Practice your pitch until it feels natural and engaging.

4. Listen and Show Interest

Effective networking involves active listening. Show genuine interest in others by asking questions and seeking to understand their perspectives and needs.

5. Follow Up Promptly

After making connections, follow up promptly with a personalized message or email. Express your gratitude for the connection and express your interest in continuing the conversation.

6. Provide Value

Networking is a two-way street. Look for opportunities to provide value to your connections. Share insights, offer assistance, or make introductions that benefit others.

7. Nurture Relationships

Building strong relationships takes time and effort. Stay in touch with your network, even when you don't have an immediate need. Check in periodically to maintain the connection.

8. Join Industry Associations or Groups
Consider joining industry associations or groups that provide opportunities for networking. These organizations often host events, conferences, and forums tailored to your field.

9. Offer to Help Organize or Speak
Volunteer to help organize events or speak at industry conferences. These roles can boost your visibility and credibility within your network.

10. Leverage Online Platforms
Social media platforms, such as LinkedIn, provide powerful tools for online networking. Use these platforms to connect with industry professionals, participate in discussions, and share your expertise.

Overcoming Networking Challenges

Networking can be daunting, especially for introverted entrepreneurs or those facing distractions in their daily lives. Here are strategies to overcome common networking challenges:

1. Set Realistic Expectations
Recognize that not every networking encounter will lead to immediate opportunities. Networking is a long-term investment in relationship building.

2. Practice Active Listening
If you're uncomfortable with small talk, focus on active listening. Ask open-ended questions that encourage others to share, and genuinely engage with their responses.

3. Attend Networking Workshops
Consider attending networking workshops or courses to build your networking skills and boost your confidence.

4. Leverage Your Strengths
Identify your unique strengths and leverage them in your network-

ing efforts. Whether it's your expertise, storytelling abilities, or problem-solving skills, your strengths can set you apart.

5. Seek Introductory Events
Look for introductory networking events where you can ease into conversations with others who may be in the same situation.

6. Follow Up Religiously
The real value of networking often lies in the follow-up. Make it a habit to follow up with your contacts promptly after an event or connection is made.

Accountability partnerships and networking are indispensable tools in the entrepreneurial toolkit. They provide essential support, insights, and resources for navigating distractions and achieving strategic goals. By cultivating effective accountability partnerships and engaging in purposeful networking, you can bolster your entrepreneurial journey and increase your likelihood of success.

In the upcoming chapters, we will continue to explore techniques and strategies to empower you on your path to overcoming distractions and realizing your entrepreneurial vision.

Chapter 10

The Art of Saying No

In the world of entrepreneurship, where opportunities beckon from every corner and distractions lurk around every turn, mastering the art of saying no is an indispensable skill. As an entrepreneur, your time, energy, and resources are finite, and your ability to safeguard them against unnecessary commitments and diversions is paramount. This chapter explores the profound importance of saying no, the challenges that entrepreneurs often face in doing so, and the strategies to gracefully decline requests, ensuring that your journey towards your strategic goals remains undeterred.

The Significance of Saying No

The act of saying no extends far beyond mere rejection; it is a profound assertion of your priorities and boundaries. Let's delve into why it holds such significance in the context of entrepreneurship:

1. Focus Preservation
Entrepreneurs live in a world teeming with opportunities and distractions. Saying no serves as a guardian of your focus, ensuring that your valuable time and attention remain directed toward what truly matters for your business.

2. Strategic Decision-Making
Every commitment you undertake comes at a cost. Each "yes" to a request or opportunity carries an inherent "no" to something else—potentially something more aligned with your strategic goals. Saying no empowers you to make deliberate, strategic choices regarding where you invest your resources.

3. Burnout Prevention
Overcommitment is a perilous path that often leads to burnout—a common affliction among entrepreneurs. By uttering no when needed, you protect your well-being, mental health, and long-term sustainability.

4. Enhanced Effectiveness
Entrepreneurs who judiciously select their commitments can allocate their time and energy to tasks that align with their strengths and expertise. This, in turn, enhances overall effectiveness and productivity.

5. Boundaries Reinforcement

Saying no is an assertion of personal and professional boundaries. It communicates that your time, resources, and energy are valuable assets that should be respected.

The Challenges of Saying No

Despite its paramount importance, saying no can be remarkably challenging, primarily due to these common hurdles entrepreneurs encounter:

1. Fear of Missing Out (FOMO)

The fear of missing out on potential opportunities, benefits, or experiences is a powerful psychological force that often leads entrepreneurs to say yes to far more than they should.

2. Desire to Please

Entrepreneurs, often seen as natural problem solvers and collaborators, have a proclivity for wanting to help others. This innate desire to please can make it arduous to decline requests.

3. External Pressure to Say Yes

External pressures, such as societal expectations, industry norms, or peer pressure, can create a perceived obligation to say yes, even when it runs contrary to your best interests.

4. Uncertainty of Outcomes

Entrepreneurs are, by nature, risk-takers, but they also seek predictability in their ventures. The uncertainty of outcomes can deter them from saying no when there's ambiguity about potential future benefits.

Strategies for Saying No Gracefully

Saying no gracefully is an art form that can be cultivated and perfected over time. These strategies can assist you in gracefully and assertively declining requests or distractions:

1. Pause and Reflect

Before hastily accepting or declining a request, pause for a moment of reflection. Consider how the commitment aligns with your strategic goals and whether it's realistically feasible within your current capacity.

2. Prioritize Your Goals

Invariably, prioritize your strategic goals when making decisions. If a request harmonizes with your objectives, it merits consideration; if not, consider declining.

3. Practice Empathetic Communication

When conveying your decision to decline, communicate with empathy and understanding. Express your appreciation for the opportunity and explain your choice thoughtfully.

4. Be Clear and Firm

Vague or ambiguous responses tend to be unhelpful. Be clear and unwavering in your decision to decline, leaving no room for misinterpretation.

5. Offer Alternatives

If feasible, propose alternatives that may be more suitable. This demonstrates your willingness to be helpful, even if you can't fulfill the specific request.

6. Use Time-Buffer Statements

Deploy time-buffer statements like, "Let me check my schedule," or "I'll need some time to think about this." These phrases grant you breathing space to evaluate the request thoroughly before committing.

7. Practice Saying No

The skill of saying no improves with practice. Start by saying no to smaller, less impactful requests and gradually work your way up to more significant commitments.

8. Set Boundaries

Establish explicit boundaries for your availability and commitments, and communicate these boundaries clearly to others so they understand your limitations.

9. Learn to Say No to Yourself
Saying no isn't solely applicable to external requests; it also pertains to self-imposed distractions and tasks that don't align with your goals. Develop the ability to say no to yourself when necessary.

10. Seek Support
Share your challenges with trusted friends, mentors, or accountability partners. They can offer guidance, insights, and hold you accountable for saying no when required.

The Transformative Impact of Saying No

Embracing the art of saying no can have a transformative influence on your entrepreneurial journey:

1. Enhanced Focus and Productivity
By saying no to distractions and peripheral commitments, you liberate your time and mental energy, which can then be invested in high-impact tasks and strategic goals. This, in turn, leads to improved focus and productivity.

2. Informed Decision-Making
With fewer commitments vying for your attention, you can make more deliberate and informed decisions. The quality of your choices is elevated, leading to more favorable outcomes.

3. Reduction in Stress and Overwhelm
Overcommitment often results in stress and overwhelm, which are detrimental to your well-being. Saying no enables you to manage your workload better and maintain a healthier work-life balance.

4. Enhanced Reputation
Being selective about your commitments can enhance your reputation as someone who values their time and resources. Others are more likely to respect your boundaries and commitments.

5. Opportunities for Growth
Saying no to certain commitments creates space for new opportunities and experiences that align with your goals and interests, fostering personal and professional growth.

Networking with Purpose

While saying no centers on managing external requests and distractions, networking with a purpose revolves around proactively seeking connections and opportunities that align with your entrepreneurial journey. Here's how to network effectively with intent:

1. Define Your Networking Objectives
Commence your networking journey by defining your objectives clearly. What are you aiming to achieve through networking? Whether it's finding mentors, securing funding, or expanding your customer base, having crystalline goals will guide your networking endeavors.

2. Identify Target Connections
Determine the individuals or groups most likely to assist you in achieving your networking goals. This may encompass industry experts, potential collaborators, or organizations closely aligned with your interests.

3. Leverage Online Platforms
Harness online platforms, such as LinkedIn or specialized industry forums, to connect with like-minded professionals and organizations. Ensure that your online presence accurately reflects your goals and expertise.

4. Attend Relevant Events
Participate actively in events, conferences, or workshops that resonate with your objectives. These gatherings offer invaluable opportunities for in-person networking and knowledge exchange.

5. Be a Valuable Resource
Approach networking with the intention of providing value to others. Share your expertise, extend assistance, and facilitate introductions when appropriate. Networking thrives on reciprocity.

6. Follow Up Strategically
After establishing connections, follow up judiciously. Dispatch personalized follow-up messages that reference your previous conversation and express your interest in future collaboration or commu-

nication.

7. Nurture Relationships
The cultivation and maintenance of relationships are pivotal in effective networking. Regularly check in with your connections, disseminate updates, and proffer your support when needed.

8. Seek Diverse Perspectives
Diversity within your network leads to diverse perspectives and opportunities. Connect with individuals hailing from varying backgrounds, industries, and experiences to broaden your horizons.

9. Stay Informed
Stay apprised of industry trends, news, and developments to engage in meaningful dialogues with your network. A well-informed stance demonstrates your dedication and expertise.

10. Evaluate and Adjust
Periodically assess the efficacy of your networking efforts. Are you making progress toward your objectives? Modify your approach as required to maximize the impact of your networking.

Overcoming Networking Challenges

Effective networking necessitates tenacity and adaptability, especially when facing common networking challenges:

1. Overcoming Shyness or Introversion
If you grapple with shyness or introversion, commence your networking journey by attending smaller, more intimate events. This gradual approach allows you to build confidence. Concentrate on one-on-one conversations and uncover common ground with others.

2. Managing Time Constraints
Entrepreneurs often grapple with time constraints due to their demanding schedules. Prioritize events and connections that align most closely with your goals. Contemplate allocating specific time slots dedicated exclusively to networking.

3. Navigating Rejections

In the world of networking, not every connection you establish will culminate in a successful partnership or opportunity. Rejections are a natural facet of the process; don't be disheartened by them. Instead, persist in your quest to forge the right connections.

4. Avoiding Inauthentic Networking

Avoid the pitfall of engaging in overly transactional or inauthentic networking. Authentic relationships, grounded in genuine connections, are more likely to lead to mutually beneficial opportunities.

Saying no and networking with purpose are two sides of the same entrepreneurial coin, integral to your ability to make informed decisions about where you invest your finite resources—be it time, energy, or attention. By mastering the art of saying no when distractions or irrelevant commitments beckon and by networking strategically to build meaningful connections, you can navigate the intricate landscape of entrepreneurship with unwavering focus, purpose, and success.

We will continue to explore techniques and strategies that empower you to conquer distractions and steadfastly advance toward your entrepreneurial vision.

Chapter 11

The Role of Self-Care in Entrepreneurship

It's easy to overlook one critical aspect of your journey—self-care. As an entrepreneur, your well-being is the foundation upon which your business stands. Neglecting self-care can lead to burnout, diminished productivity, and a weakened capacity to navigate the inevitable distractions and challenges that come your way. In this chapter, we'll explore the pivotal role of self-care in entrepreneurship, why it's not a luxury but a necessity, and actionable strategies to integrate it into your entrepreneurial life.

The Crucial Role of Self-Care

Self-care isn't a self-indulgent luxury; it's a fundamental necessity for entrepreneurs. Here's why it plays such a pivotal role:

1. Burnout Prevention
Entrepreneurship is a demanding journey that can easily lead to burnout—a state of emotional, physical, and mental exhaustion. Self-care acts as a shield against burnout, preserving your resilience and energy.

2. Enhanced Resilience
Resilience is your capacity to bounce back from setbacks and challenges. Prioritizing self-care fortifies your resilience, enabling you to confront distractions and setbacks with greater fortitude.

3. Mental Clarity
A well-rested and nurtured mind is sharper and more agile. Self-care fosters mental clarity, allowing you to make informed decisions and remain focused on your strategic goals.

4. Improved Creativity
Creativity is the lifeblood of entrepreneurship. Self-care nurtures your creative spirit, enabling you to devise innovative solutions and navigate distractions with ingenuity.

5. Physical Well-Being
Your physical health is a cornerstone of your entrepreneurial journey. Self-care practices that promote physical well-being keep you in prime condition to tackle challenges.

The Myth of Endless Hustle

The entrepreneurial world often perpetuates the myth of endless hustle—relentless work, long hours, and minimal rest. However, this approach is unsustainable and counterproductive. Here's why:

1. Diminished Productivity
Continuously pushing yourself without breaks leads to diminishing returns. Fatigue sets in, diminishing your productivity and decision-making abilities.

2. Increased Error Rates
Exhaustion elevates the likelihood of making costly errors in judgment and execution, potentially exacerbating distractions and setbacks.

3. Negative Impact on Health
Neglecting self-care can have dire consequences for your physical and mental health, ultimately undermining your entrepreneurial journey.

4. Strained Relationships
Excessive work can strain personal relationships, further complicating your ability to navigate distractions and challenges effectively.

Strategies for Effective Self-Care

Self-care is a holistic endeavor encompassing physical, mental, emotional, and social well-being. Here are actionable strategies to integrate effective self-care into your entrepreneurial life:

1. Prioritize Sleep
Adequate sleep is non-negotiable for well-being. Prioritize a consistent sleep schedule and create a restful sleep environment to ensure you wake up refreshed and ready to tackle distractions.

2. Exercise Regularly
Physical activity boosts your energy levels, enhances mental clarity, and reduces stress. Incorporate regular exercise into your routine to bolster your physical and mental resilience.

3. Practice Mindfulness and Meditation

Mindfulness and meditation practices cultivate mental clarity and emotional well-being. Dedicate time each day to these practices to sharpen your focus and calm distractions.

4. Set Boundaries

Establish boundaries around your work hours and personal time. Communicate these boundaries to clients, colleagues, and yourself to protect your time for self-care.

5. Nurture Your Interests

Engage in hobbies and interests outside of work. These activities provide an essential mental break and can reignite your creativity.

6. Seek Support

Don't hesitate to seek support from friends, family, or a therapist. Entrepreneurship can be isolating, and seeking guidance or simply having someone to talk to can alleviate stress.

7. Disconnect Regularly

Periodically disconnect from digital devices and work-related communications. This digital detox allows you to recharge and reduces the constant distractions of technology.

8. Delegate and Outsource

Recognize that you don't have to do everything yourself. Delegate tasks that are not your strengths or that can be outsourced, allowing you to focus on your core competencies.

9. Practice Gratitude

Cultivate gratitude as a daily practice. Reflect on the positive aspects of your entrepreneurial journey and life in general. Gratitude can boost your resilience and overall well-being.

10. Set Realistic Goals

Set achievable and realistic goals for your business. Unrealistic expectations can lead to chronic stress and distract you from meaningful progress.

Integrating Self-Care into Your Routine

Effectively integrating self-care into your entrepreneurial routine requires commitment and discipline. Here's how you can make self-care a habitual part of your life:

1. Create a Self-Care Schedule
Allocate specific time slots for self-care activities in your calendar. Treat these appointments with the same level of importance as business meetings.

2. Set Reminders
Use digital reminders or alarms to prompt you to engage in self-care practices throughout the day. These reminders help break up your work and encourage self-care.

3. Track Your Progress
Keep a journal or use digital tools to track your self-care activities. Regularly reviewing your progress can motivate you to stay consistent.

4. Accountability Partners
Partner with a friend or colleague who values self-care. Share your self-care goals and hold each other accountable for maintaining these practices.

5. Celebrate Small Wins
Acknowledge and celebrate your self-care achievements. Small wins in self-care contribute to overall well-being and can help you better manage distractions and challenges.

Self-Care as a
Distraction Management Strategy

Self-care isn't just about feeling better; it's a strategic tool for managing distractions and challenges in your entrepreneurial journey. Here's how self-care can enhance your ability to stay focused and resilient:

1. Stress Reduction

Self-care practices reduce stress, making it easier to remain composed and focused when distractions arise.

2. Improved Concentration

A well-rested and nurtured mind is more capable of sustaining focus and resisting the allure of distractions.

3. Enhanced Problem-Solving

Self-care sharpens your mental faculties, enabling you to tackle challenges and distractions with increased creativity and effectiveness.

4. Resilience Building

Regular self-care builds your resilience, allowing you to bounce back from setbacks and disruptions more swiftly.

5. Balanced Decision-Making

Self-care fosters emotional balance, which is essential for making sound, rational decisions in the face of distractions or unexpected challenges.

Cultivating a Culture of Self-Care

As an entrepreneur, you have the opportunity to cultivate a culture of self-care within your business. This not only benefits you but also your team. Here's how to foster a self-care culture:

1. Lead by Example

Demonstrate the importance of self-care by prioritizing it in your own life. Your actions set the tone for your team.

2. Encourage Open Dialogue

Create an environment where team members feel comfortable discussing self-care and well-being. Encourage open dialogue about managing stress and distractions.

3. Offer Resources

Provide resources and opportunities for self-care, such as access to wellness programs, mental health support, or flexible work arrangements.

4. Respect Boundaries

Respect the boundaries of your team members. Avoid sending work-related messages or requests outside of business hours, and encourage others to do the same.

5. Recognize and Reward Self-Care

Acknowledge and reward team members who prioritize self-care. Celebrate their efforts to maintain well-being.

Self-care isn't a luxury; it's a strategic imperative for entrepreneurs. By prioritizing your physical, mental, and emotional well-being, you fortify your resilience, enhance your ability to manage distractions, and optimize your overall performance. Embrace self-care as an integral part of your entrepreneurial journey, and watch how it transforms your capacity to navigate the challenges and distractions that lie ahead.

As we proceed to the subsequent chapters, we'll delve deeper into techniques and strategies that empower you to overcome distractions, stay focused on your strategic goals, and lead a fulfilling entrepreneurial life.

Chapter 12

Overcoming Burnout in Entrepreneurship

Entrepreneurship is a thrilling journey filled with exhilarating highs and daunting challenges. As you navigate the entrepreneurial landscape, it's not uncommon to encounter a formidable adversary: burnout. Burnout is more than just feeling tired or stressed; it's a state of emotional, physical, and mental exhaustion that can have a detrimental impact on your well-being and your ability to achieve your strategic goals. In this chapter, we will explore the insidious nature of burnout in entrepreneurship, its warning signs, and practical strategies to overcome it and reclaim your passion for your business.

The Menace of Burnout

Burnout is a silent predator that can gradually creep into your entrepreneurial life, sapping your energy and enthusiasm. Understanding the nature of this adversary is the first step in overcoming it:

1. Gradual Erosion
Burnout doesn't strike suddenly; it erodes your well-being over time. It often begins with a sense of overwhelm and intensifies as you persistently push your limits.

2. Physical and Emotional Toll
Burnout takes a toll on your body and mind. It can manifest as chronic fatigue, insomnia, irritability, and a sense of hopelessness.

3. Impact on Performance
Burnout hampers your performance. You may find it challenging to concentrate, make decisions, or remain motivated, making it difficult to stay focused on your strategic goals.

4. Strained Relationships
The effects of burnout extend to your personal life. You may become less engaged in relationships, leading to strains in your personal and professional connections.

Recognizing the Signs of Burnout

Detecting burnout in its early stages is critical to preventing its progression. Here are common signs to watch for:

1. Chronic Fatigue
Feeling persistently tired, even after a full night's sleep, is a classic sign of burnout.

2. Loss of Motivation
A sudden loss of interest and motivation in your business, which once excited you, can be a red flag.

3. Decreased Performance
A noticeable decline in your performance, productivity, and decision-making abilities may indicate burnout.

4. Cynicism and Negativity
Becoming increasingly cynical, negative, or critical towards your work or others is a warning sign.

5. Insomnia or Sleep Disturbances
Difficulty falling asleep or staying asleep can be a consequence of burnout-related stress.

6. Physical Symptoms
Frequent headaches, digestive problems, and other physical symptoms can accompany burnout.

7. Withdrawal from Relationships
Avoiding social interactions, both personally and professionally, is common among those experiencing burnout.

The Impact of Burnout on Distractions

Burnout and distractions are closely intertwined. When you're burnt out, distractions become more potent and challenging to manage:

1. Diminished Focus
Burnout saps your ability to focus, making it easier for distractions to pull you away from your strategic goals.

2. Increased Procrastination
Burnout often leads to procrastination, as you may find it difficult to summon the motivation to tackle important tasks.

3. Elevated Stress Levels
Distractions can exacerbate stress, which is already heightened in the presence of burnout.

4. Impaired Decision-Making
Burnout impairs your decision-making abilities, making it harder to discern which distractions to prioritize or reject.

5. Decreased Resilience
Burnout diminishes your resilience to distractions, making you more susceptible to their allure.

Strategies to Overcome Burnout

Overcoming burnout is a multifaceted process that requires commitment and self-awareness. Here are actionable strategies to help you reclaim your passion for your business and overcome burnout:

1. Acknowledge Burnout
Recognize and accept that you are experiencing burnout. Denial can exacerbate the problem.

2. Seek Support
Don't face burnout alone. Reach out to friends, family, or a therapist for support and guidance.

3. Set Boundaries
Establish clear boundaries between work and personal life. Make a conscious effort to disconnect from work-related activities during personal time.

4. Practice Self-Care
Prioritize self-care activities, including exercise, mindfulness, and adequate sleep, to nurture your physical and mental well-being.

5. Delegate and Outsource
Identify tasks that can be delegated or outsourced to reduce your workload and minimize stress.

6. Reevaluate Goals
Review your business goals and consider whether they align with your values and passion. Adjust your goals if necessary to reignite your enthusiasm.

7. Time Management
Implement effective time management techniques to prioritize tasks and reduce the sense of overwhelm.

8. Say No Gracefully
Practice the art of saying no to commitments and distractions that do not align with your strategic goals.

9. Disconnect Regularly
Set aside time to disconnect from digital devices and work-related communication to recharge your mental and emotional batteries.

10. Hire a Coach or Mentor
Consider hiring a coach or mentor who can provide guidance, accountability, and a fresh perspective on your business.

Strategies to Manage Distractions During Burnout

While overcoming burnout is paramount, it's equally important to manage distractions effectively during this process. Here are strategies to help you do just that:

1. Prioritize Self-Care
Make self-care a top priority to mitigate the impact of distractions during burnout recovery.

2. Set Clear Goals
Define clear and specific goals to guide your work and help you stay focused on your strategic objectives.

3. Use Time Management Techniques

Employ time management techniques, such as the Pomodoro Technique or the Eisenhower Matrix, to structure your work and reduce distractions.

4. Practice Mindfulness

Mindfulness exercises can enhance your ability to stay present and minimize the pull of distractions.

5. Create a Distraction-Free Environment

Designate a dedicated workspace that minimizes distractions, both physical and digital.

6. Limit Multitasking

Resist the temptation to multitask, as it can fragment your attention and amplify the impact of distractions.

7. Utilize Productivity Tools

Leverage productivity tools and apps that can help you stay organized and on track.

The Journey to Renewed Passion

Overcoming burnout and managing distractions is a journey that requires patience and self-compassion. As you implement these strategies, remember that recovery is a gradual process, and setbacks may occur. Here's what to expect on your path to renewed passion for your business:

1. Early Resistance

Initially, you may encounter resistance to change, both from within yourself and from external factors. Stay committed to your well-being.

2. Small Wins

Celebrate small victories along the way. Each day that you effectively manage distractions and prioritize self-care is a step toward recovery.

3. Rekindled Enthusiasm

As burnout recedes, you'll likely notice a rekindling of your enthusiasm and passion for your business.

4. Enhanced Focus

With improved well-being and effective distraction management, your ability to stay focused on your strategic goals will strengthen.

5. Sustainable Success

By conquering burnout and mastering distractions, you pave the way for sustainable success in your entrepreneurial journey.

Cultivating Resilience for the Long Haul

Burnout is a potent reminder of the importance of resilience in entrepreneurship. Resilience is not just about bouncing back from adversity; it's about proactively safeguarding your well-being and capacity to achieve your strategic goals. Here are enduring principles for cultivating resilience:

1. Self-Care as a Habit

Make self-care a lifelong habit, not just a reaction to burnout. Regular self-care routines fortify your resilience.

2. Continuous Adaptation

Entrepreneurship is dynamic, requiring constant adaptation. Cultivate adaptability as a core competency to navigate distractions and challenges effectively.

3. Embrace Learning

View setbacks and distractions as opportunities for growth and learning. Each experience can strengthen your resilience.

4. Lean on Support Networks

Maintain strong support networks of friends, mentors, and peers who can provide guidance and encouragement during challenging times.

5. Celebrate Progress

Celebrate your progress and successes, no matter how small. Acknowledging your achievements bolsters your resilience.

Overcoming burnout and managing distractions are interwoven challenges in entrepreneurship. By recognizing the signs of burnout, seeking support, and implementing effective self-care and distraction management strategies, you can rekindle your passion for your business and regain your focus on strategic goals.

As we move forward into the subsequent chapters, we will delve deeper into techniques and strategies to empower you to conquer distractions, navigate challenges, and achieve your entrepreneurial aspirations with renewed vitality and purpose.

Chapter 13

Strategies for Handling Unexpected Distractions in Entrepreneurship

Unexpected distractions are an inevitability. No matter how well you plan and organize, unforeseen disruptions can disrupt your flow, hinder your productivity, and throw you off course. To navigate these unexpected distractions effectively, you need a set of strategies and techniques that can help you stay focused on your strategic goals. In this chapter, we'll explore the nature of unexpected distractions in entrepreneurship, why they can be particularly challenging, and actionable strategies to handle them with composure and resilience.

The Nature of Unexpected Distractions

Unexpected distractions in entrepreneurship can take many forms, from urgent client requests to technical glitches, and even personal emergencies. Here's why they can be especially disruptive:

1. Disruption of Flow
Unexpected distractions disrupt your workflow and can take you out of the zone where you're most productive and focused.

2. Time Drain
Dealing with unexpected distractions often consumes valuable time that could be better spent on strategic tasks.

3. Stress and Frustration
Frequent and unmanaged distractions can lead to increased stress and frustration, affecting your overall well-being.

4. Impact on Decision-Making
Handling unexpected distractions can fragment your attention and hinder your ability to make sound decisions.

The Challenges of Handling Unexpected Distractions

Entrepreneurs face specific challenges when it comes to handling unexpected distractions:

1. High Responsibility
Entrepreneurs often bear significant responsibility for the success

of their businesses, making it challenging to delegate or ignore unexpected distractions.

2. Resource Constraints

Smaller businesses may lack the resources to hire staff specifically dedicated to handling distractions, leaving entrepreneurs to manage them personally.

3. Entrepreneurial Mindset

The entrepreneurial mindset is often characterized by a willingness to seize opportunities quickly, which can lead to impulsive responses to unexpected distractions.

4. Balancing Priorities

Entrepreneurs must juggle multiple responsibilities, making it difficult to balance unexpected distractions with strategic goals.

Strategies for Handling
Unexpected Distractions

Effectively handling unexpected distractions requires a combination of proactive planning and on-the-spot strategies. Here are actionable techniques to help you manage these disruptions:

1. Prevent When Possible

While not all distractions can be foreseen, some can be prevented with proactive measures. Identify common sources of distractions in your business and take steps to mitigate them. For example, implement backup systems to prevent technical issues or establish clear communication protocols with clients to manage their expectations.

2. Prioritize and Delegate

When unexpected distractions arise, quickly assess their importance and urgency. If a distraction is critical, prioritize it. If it can be delegated to a team member or outsourced, do so to free up your time for more strategic tasks.

3. Time Blocking

Implement time blocking techniques to create dedicated blocks of time for focused work. These blocks act as a buffer against unexpected distractions and ensure you have uninterrupted periods for strategic tasks.

4. Have a Contingency Plan

Develop contingency plans for common disruptions. For example, if you often face technical issues, have a backup device or internet connection ready. If client emergencies are common, establish a clear process for addressing them efficiently.

5. Communication Protocol

Create a communication protocol for your team and clients that outlines expectations for responding to urgent matters. Having a structured approach to handling unexpected demands can streamline the process.

6. Mindfulness Practices

Practice mindfulness techniques, such as deep breathing or meditation, to maintain composure when unexpected distractions occur. These practices can help you stay calm and focused.

7. Set Boundaries

Establish clear boundaries around your work hours and availability. Communicate these boundaries to clients, colleagues, and team members so they understand when you can be reached for non-urgent matters.

8. Avoid Multitasking

Resist the temptation to multitask when handling unexpected distractions. Instead, focus on addressing the distraction efficiently before returning to your primary task. Multitasking can lead to errors and increased stress.

9. Embrace the 2-Minute Rule

If a distraction can be resolved in two minutes or less, address it immediately. This rule can help you quickly eliminate minor disruptions without derailing your workflow.

10. Learn from Each Distraction

View each unexpected distraction as an opportunity to learn and improve your processes. After the distraction is resolved, take a moment to reflect on what caused it and how you can prevent similar disruptions in the future.

Maintaining Focus on Strategic Goals

Successfully handling unexpected distractions is essential, but maintaining focus on your strategic goals is equally important. Here's how to ensure that unexpected disruptions don't derail your long-term objectives:

1. Stay Agile
While it's important to remain committed to your strategic goals, be agile in your approach. Adapt to unexpected disruptions by adjusting your priorities and strategies as needed.

2. Regularly Review Goals
Frequently review your strategic goals to ensure they remain relevant and aligned with your vision. This can help you stay motivated and on track, even when dealing with distractions.

3. Delegate Effectively
Delegate tasks and responsibilities to team members who can handle them competently. Effective delegation frees up your time and mental energy to focus on strategic tasks.

4. Use Technology Wisely
Leverage technology to streamline your workflow and minimize distractions. Use productivity tools and apps to automate repetitive tasks and manage your schedule efficiently.

5. Reevaluate Priorities
When faced with unexpected distractions, reevaluate your priorities and make conscious decisions about where to allocate your time and resources to minimize the impact on your strategic goals.

6. Seek Support
Lean on your support network, including mentors, advisors, and peers, for guidance and advice on how to maintain focus on your strategic objectives during disruptions.

The Role of Resilience

Resilience is a critical attribute for handling unexpected distractions and maintaining focus on your strategic goals. Here's how resilience can help:

1. Adaptability
Resilience enables you to adapt to changing circumstances and disruptions, finding new ways to achieve your strategic goals.

2. Mental Toughness
Resilience builds mental toughness, allowing you to stay determined and focused on your long-term objectives, even in the face of distractions.

3. Stress Management
Resilience equips you with the tools to manage stress effectively, which is crucial when handling unexpected disruptions.

4. Quick Recovery
Resilience helps you bounce back quickly from distractions and setbacks, minimizing their impact on your progress.

Handling unexpected distractions is a fundamental skill for every entrepreneur. By implementing proactive measures, setting boundaries, and practicing mindfulness, you can manage these disruptions with composure and minimize their impact on your strategic goals. Remember that resilience is your ally in navigating the dynamic world of entrepreneurship. As we move forward into the subsequent chapters, we will continue to explore techniques and strategies that empower you to conquer distractions, stay focused on your strategic goals, and achieve entrepreneurial success.

Chapter 14

Measuring Progress and Adapting in Entrepreneurship

Entrepreneurship is a journey filled with twists, turns, and the unexpected. To navigate this dynamic landscape effectively, you need more than just a clear vision and strategic goals; you also need the ability to measure your progress and adjust your course when necessary. In this chapter, we will explore the importance of measuring progress in entrepreneurship, the key metrics and indicators to track, and how to adapt your strategies to stay on the path to success.

The Significance of Measuring Progress

Measuring progress is not merely an administrative task; it is a fundamental element of successful entrepreneurship. Here's why it matters:

1. Clarity and Direction
Regular progress measurement provides clarity on whether you are moving in the right direction toward your strategic goals or if adjustments are needed.

2. Accountability
Tracking progress holds you accountable for the goals you've set. It motivates you to stay on track and meet your objectives.

3. Identifying Success
Measuring progress allows you to celebrate your successes along the way, reinforcing your confidence and determination.

4. Early Detection of Issues
Progress measurement can reveal early signs of potential problems or setbacks, enabling you to address them proactively.

Key Metrics for Entrepreneurial Progress

To measure progress effectively, you need to identify and track key metrics and indicators relevant to your specific business and goals. Here are some common categories of metrics to consider:

1. Financial Metrics

Revenue and Profitability: Track your revenue and profit margins to ensure they align with your financial goals.

Cash Flow: Monitor cash flow to maintain financial stability and liquidity.

Expenses: Keep a close eye on expenses to identify cost-saving opportunities.

Return on Investment (ROI): Evaluate the effectiveness of your investments and marketing campaigns.

2. Customer Metrics

Customer Acquisition Cost (CAC): Calculate the cost of acquiring each customer to ensure it is within acceptable limits.

Customer Lifetime Value (CLV): Assess the long-term value of your customers to guide marketing and retention efforts.

Customer Satisfaction: Gather feedback and measure customer satisfaction to identify areas for improvement.

3. Operational Metrics

Efficiency: Evaluate the efficiency of your operations by measuring key processes and workflows.

Inventory Management: Monitor inventory turnover and levels to optimize supply chain management.

Quality Control: Track product or service quality to ensure it meets customer expectations.

4. Marketing and Sales Metrics

Conversion Rates: Measure the percentage of leads or prospects that convert into customers.

Website Traffic: Analyze website traffic data to assess the effectiveness of online marketing efforts.

Lead Generation: Monitor the success of lead generation strategies and campaigns.

5. Strategic Metrics

Goal Achievement: Regularly assess your progress toward achieving your strategic goals.

Market Share: Determine your market share relative to competitors and industry benchmarks.

Brand Recognition: Measure brand awareness and recognition among your target audience.

Setting Clear Milestones

In addition to tracking ongoing metrics, it's crucial to set clear milestones and checkpoints along your entrepreneurial journey. Milestones serve as tangible markers of progress and provide you with specific goals to work towards. Here's how to set and utilize milestones effectively:

1. Define Specific Milestones
Milestones should be specific, measurable, achievable, relevant, and time-bound (SMART). They should represent significant achievements or turning points in your business.

2. Align Milestones with Goals
Each milestone should align with one or more of your strategic goals. This alignment ensures that achieving milestones contributes directly to your overarching objectives.

3. Establish Timeframes
Assign realistic timeframes for reaching each milestone. Timeframes create a sense of urgency and help you allocate resources efficiently.

4. Monitor Progress Toward Milestones
Regularly assess your progress toward achieving milestones. Consider creating a visual representation, such as a Gantt chart or a progress dashboard, to track milestones visually.

5. Celebrate Milestone Achievements
Celebrate your achievements when you reach milestones. Acknowledging your progress reinforces your commitment to your goals and boosts morale.

Adapting Strategies and Course Corrections

Measuring progress isn't solely about tracking metrics and achieving milestones; it also involves the ability to adapt and make course corrections when necessary. Here's how to navigate changes effectively:

1. Continuous Assessment
Regularly assess your business environment, market conditions, and internal factors that may impact your progress. Stay informed and vigilant.

2. Identify Signals for Change
Look for signals that suggest a need for adjustment. These signals may include declining sales, shifts in customer preferences, or emerging competitors.

3. Stay Agile
Maintain an agile mindset that is open to change and willing to pivot when required. Be flexible and responsive to new information.

4. Engage Stakeholders
Involve key stakeholders, such as team members, advisors, and mentors, in discussions about potential course corrections. Their insights can be invaluable.

5. Evaluate Risks and Rewards
Before making significant changes, conduct a thorough risk-reward analysis. Consider the potential benefits and drawbacks of each

course of action.

6. Plan for Contingencies
Develop contingency plans that outline how you will respond to different scenarios or challenges. Having a plan in place can reduce uncertainty and anxiety.

7. Implement Changes Gradually
If major course corrections are necessary, consider implementing them gradually to minimize disruption and evaluate their impact incrementally.

8. Communicate Transparently
Maintain transparent communication with your team, customers, and stakeholders during times of change. Clear communication fosters trust and alignment.

9. Monitor and Measure Results
After making course corrections, closely monitor the results to determine if they are achieving the desired outcomes. Be prepared to adjust further if needed.

Balancing Persistence and Adaptation

In entrepreneurship, finding the right balance between persistence and adaptation is essential. While it's crucial to stay committed to your strategic goals, it's equally important to recognize when a change in direction is necessary. Here's how to strike that balance:

1. Stay Committed to Core Values
Maintain a steadfast commitment to your core values and principles, which should guide your decision-making even when adapting to new circumstances.

2. Evaluate Feedback and Data
Use feedback from customers, market research, and performance metrics to inform your decisions. Data-driven insights can help you make informed course corrections.

3. Don't Fear Failure
Embrace the possibility of failure as a potential outcome of entrepreneurial experimentation. Failure can lead to valuable lessons and insights.

4. Seek Guidance
Consult with mentors, advisors, and industry experts to gain perspective and insights that can inform your decisions.

5. Stay Resilient
Maintain resilience in the face of setbacks and challenges. Entrepreneurship is a journey filled with ups and downs, and persistence often pays off in the long run.

6. Be Adaptable
Cultivate adaptability as a core entrepreneurial skill. The ability to pivot and adjust your strategies can be a powerful asset.

Measuring progress and adapting in entrepreneurship are not just practices; they are vital skills that can make the difference between success and stagnation. By diligently tracking key metrics, setting clear milestones, and remaining open to course corrections, you can navigate the complexities of entrepreneurship with confidence and resilience. As we proceed into the subsequent chapters, we will delve deeper into techniques and strategies that empower you to conquer distractions, adapt to changing circumstances, and achieve your entrepreneurial aspirations with unwavering determination.

Chapter 15

Success Stories and Insights in Entrepreneurship

Success in entrepreneurship is not a solitary journey but a collective effort that draws inspiration from the experiences and achievements of those who have walked the path before us. In this chapter, we'll explore a selection of success stories and glean valuable insights from the journeys of accomplished entrepreneurs. These stories serve as beacons of inspiration, offering lessons, motivation, and a glimpse into the diverse approaches that have led to entrepreneurial triumph.

Success Story 1
Robert F. Smith - Tech Investor and Philanthropist

Robert F. Smith, a tech investor and philanthropist, is known for his remarkable success in the world of finance and his commitment to giving back to his community.

Key Insights from Robert F. Smith's Journey

Strategic Investments: Smith's success lies in his ability to make strategic investments and identify opportunities in the tech and finance sectors.

Philanthropy as a Legacy: He emphasizes the importance of using success as a platform for positive change, as demonstrated by his pledge to eliminate student loan debt for Morehouse College graduates.

Diversity and Inclusion: Smith advocates for diversity and inclusion in the tech industry, highlighting the value of diverse perspectives and talents.

Lifelong Learning: His commitment to continuous learning and adaptability has allowed him to stay ahead in an ever-evolving industry.

Success Story 2
Oprah Winfrey - A Media Mogul
and Philanthropist

Oprah Winfrey, a media mogul, talk show host, and philanthropist, is a source of inspiration for her transformative journey from a challenging upbringing to becoming one of the most influential figures in media and philanthropy.

Key Insights from Oprah Winfrey's Journey

Authenticity: Oprah's authenticity and vulnerability in sharing her personal struggles and triumphs on her talk show connected deeply with her audience.

Leveraging Adversity: She leveraged her early experiences of adversity and trauma to fuel her determination to succeed and to empathize with others.

Purpose-Driven Career: Oprah's commitment to using her platform for meaningful conversations and social impact showcases the significance of aligning one's career with a higher purpose.

Continuous Growth: Throughout her career, Oprah has demonstrated a commitment to personal growth and self-improvement, constantly seeking ways to evolve and learn.

Giving Back: Her philanthropic endeavors, including the Oprah Winfrey Leadership Academy for Girls in South Africa, reflect the profound impact an individual can have on the lives of others.

Success Story 3
Jeff Bezos - Amazon's
E-Commerce Revolution

Jeff Bezos, the founder of Amazon, has redefined e-commerce and transformed the way we shop. His entrepreneurial journey emphasizes the importance of innovation, customer-centricity, and long-term thinking.

Key Insights from Jeff Bezos's Journey

Customer Obsession: Bezos's relentless focus on meeting customer needs and enhancing the customer experience has been central to Amazon's success.

Long-Term Perspective: His willingness to forgo short-term profits in pursuit of long-term goals exemplifies the value of visionary thinking.

Innovation Culture: Bezos cultivated a culture of innovation within Amazon, encouraging employees to experiment and take calculated risks.

Adaptability: He adapted Amazon from an online bookstore into a diverse e-commerce giant and cloud computing powerhouse, showcasing the importance of adaptability in entrepreneurship.

Resilience and Persistence: Bezos's ability to persevere through early challenges, including the dot-com bubble burst, demonstrates the resilience required to build a transformative business.

Success Story 4
Madam C.J. Walker - Pioneer in Beauty and Entrepreneurship

Madam C.J. Walker, a pioneering African American entrepreneur in the early 20th century, built a beauty and haircare empire that empowered countless women and shattered racial and gender barriers.

Key Insights from Madam C.J. Walker's Journey

Entrepreneurial Tenacity: Despite facing racial discrimination and economic challenges, Madam C.J. Walker's determination and entrepreneurial spirit led to her success.

Empowering Others: She actively sought to empower other African American women by providing job opportunities and promoting financial independence.

Innovation and Product Development: Walker's commitment to product innovation and quality set her brand apart, demonstrating the importance of delivering value to customers.

Community Engagement: Her involvement in social and political causes underscores the significance of entrepreneurs engaging with and advocating for their communities.

Success Story 5
Richard Branson - The Maverick Entrepreneur

Richard Branson, the founder of the Virgin Group, is a maverick entrepreneur known for his adventurous spirit and diverse business ventures. His journey illustrates the value of risk-taking, innovation, and resilience.

Key Insights from Richard Branson's Journey

Risk-Taking: Branson's willingness to take calculated risks, such as launching Virgin Galactic, demonstrates the boldness required to pursue entrepreneurial dreams.

Customer-Centric Approach: He emphasizes the importance of putting customers first and creating experiences that delight them.

Adaptability: Branson's ability to pivot and diversify the Virgin Group's portfolio in response to changing market dynamics showcases adaptability.

Resilience in the Face of Setbacks: He has faced setbacks, including the failure of Virgin Cola, but has always bounced back with renewed determination.

Societal Impact: Branson's commitment to addressing global challenges, such as climate change, underscores the role entrepreneurs can play in driving positive change.

Common Themes and Lessons from Success Stories

While each success story is unique, several common themes and lessons emerge from these entrepreneurial journeys:

1. Vision and Purpose: Successful entrepreneurs have a clear vision and a sense of purpose that guides their actions and decisions.

2. Resilience: They display resilience in the face of adversity, learning from failures and setbacks to emerge stronger.

3. Innovation: Entrepreneurial success often hinges on innovation, whether it's in product development, business models, or customer experiences.

4. Customer-Centricity: A strong focus on understanding and serving customer needs is a common thread among successful entrepreneurs.

5. Adaptability: Entrepreneurs must be adaptable, willing to pivot when necessary, and open to new opportunities.

6. Risk-Taking: Calculated risk-taking is essential, with successful entrepreneurs being unafraid to venture into the unknown.

7. Giving Back: Many successful entrepreneurs use their wealth and influence to make a positive impact on society through philanthropy and social initiatives.

Applying Insights
to Your Entrepreneurial Journey

As you reflect on these success stories and the lessons they offer, consider how you can apply these insights to your own entrepreneurial journey:

1. Clarify Your Vision: Ensure your entrepreneurial endeavors align with a clear vision and purpose that inspire and guide you.

2. Embrace Resilience: Develop the resilience to overcome challenges and setbacks, viewing them as opportunities for growth.

3. Cultivate Innovation: Foster an innovative mindset in your business, seeking creative solutions to problems and exploring new opportunities.

4. Prioritize Customers: Place the needs and satisfaction of your customers at the forefront of your business strategy.

5. Adapt and Pivot: Be open to adapting your strategies and seizing new opportunities as your business evolves.

6. Calculated Risk-Taking: Assess risks carefully and be willing to take calculated risks that align with your goals.

7. Give Back: Consider how you can make a positive impact on your community or industry through philanthropic efforts or initiatives that drive positive change.

Success stories in entrepreneurship remind us that the journey is filled with challenges, triumphs, and opportunities for growth. By drawing inspiration from the experiences of accomplished entrepreneurs and applying the lessons they offer, you can navigate your own entrepreneurial path with confidence and determination. As we conclude this book, remember that your unique journey is still unfolding, and with the right mindset and strategies, you can achieve the success you aspire to in your entrepreneurial pursuits.

Epilogue

Embracing Your Entrepreneurial Journey

As we bring this book to a close, we embark on the final leg of our journey together—an exploration of the essential truths and enduring wisdom that underscore the entrepreneurial path. The epilogue serves as a compass, guiding you toward a deeper understanding of the challenges, rewards, and principles that define your journey as an entrepreneur. Here, we reflect on the journey you've undertaken, the wisdom you've acquired, and the boundless potential that lies ahead.

The Entrepreneurial Odyssey

The entrepreneurial journey is not a straightforward path but rather a winding odyssey filled with unexpected twists and turns. Along the way, you've encountered the formidable challenges of distractions, burnout, and unexpected disruptions. You've harnessed the power of vision, resilience, innovation, and adaptability to navigate these challenges. You've gleaned insights from the stories of accomplished entrepreneurs who have blazed trails before you.

Your journey is a testament to your courage, determination, and unwavering commitment to your entrepreneurial aspirations. It's a testament to the countless hours of hard work, the sleepless nights, and the bold decisions that have brought you to this point. And it's a testament to your vision—the driving force that propels you forward, even in the face of adversity.

The Ever-Evolving Landscape of Entrepreneurship

Entrepreneurship is not a static landscape; it's a dynamic and ever-evolving terrain. As an entrepreneur, you are both a navigator and an architect, charting your course and shaping the future. In this epilogue, we consider several fundamental truths that illuminate the essence of entrepreneurship.

1. The Pursuit of Purpose

At the heart of every successful entrepreneurial journey lies a profound sense of purpose. Purpose is the compass that guides your decisions, motivates your actions, and sustains your determination. It is the "why" that fuels your entrepreneurial spirit and gives meaning to your endeavors. Whether you seek to solve a pressing problem, create innovative solutions, or make a positive impact, your sense of purpose infuses your journey with purposefulness.

2. The Nature of Uncertainty

Uncertainty is an inherent aspect of entrepreneurship. It lurks at every corner, from market fluctuations to unforeseen challenges. Yet, it is precisely in the face of uncertainty that entrepreneurs thrive. Your ability to embrace ambiguity, adapt to change, and forge ahead with determination defines your capacity to succeed in an ever-changing world.

3. The Power of Innovation

Innovation is the engine of entrepreneurial progress. It fuels your ability to solve complex problems, disrupt industries, and create value. It is the embodiment of creativity and the driving force behind transformative ventures. As an entrepreneur, you are a catalyst for innovation, continually seeking new ways to improve, adapt, and grow.

4. The Resilience Factor

Resilience is the armor that shields you from the blows of setbacks and challenges. It's the unwavering belief in your ability to bounce back, learn from failures, and persevere. Resilience allows you to confront adversity with grace and determination, emerging stronger and more prepared for what lies ahead.

5. The Community of Entrepreneurs

Entrepreneurship is not a solitary endeavor but a community-driven pursuit. Your network of mentors, advisors, peers, and supporters forms a vital ecosystem that nurtures your growth. The wisdom and insights shared among entrepreneurs create a reservoir of knowledge that propels the collective entrepreneurial spirit forward.

The Lessons of Distraction and Focus

Throughout this book, we've explored the twin themes of distraction and focus—two forces that exert a profound influence on your entrepreneurial journey. Distractions, in their myriad forms, can derail your progress, fragment your attention, and hinder your ability to reach your strategic goals. They are the siren song that lures you away from your path.

On the flip side, focus is your anchor, your guiding star. It is the laser-like concentration that allows you to channel your energies toward what truly matters—the realization of your vision. As you've discovered, focus is not just a skill; it's a mindset, a discipline, and a way of life for the successful entrepreneur.

Distractions may persist, but so too can your commitment to resist them. By implementing the strategies and techniques outlined in this book, you've armed yourself with the tools to manage distractions effectively. You've cultivated the habits of mindfulness, time management, and resilience that are the bedrock of a distraction-resistant mindset.

The Dance with Burnout

Burnout, that formidable foe, has also made its appearance in our journey. It is the consequence of relentless effort without respite, a reminder that the pursuit of success should not come at the expense of well-being. Burnout is a signal—a call to reassess priorities, to rekindle the flames of passion, and to prioritize self-care.

In your journey, you've learned that burnout is not a sign of weakness but a reflection of your commitment to your goals. It is a testament to your dedication. Yet, it is also a reminder that balance and self-care are the cornerstones of sustained success.

The Imperative of Adaptation

Adaptation is the lifeblood of entrepreneurship. It is the ability to pivot when circumstances change, to embrace new opportunities, and to evolve with the evolving landscape. The stories of successful entrepreneurs have underscored the importance of adaptability, of seeing change not as a threat but as a canvas upon which to paint new possibilities.

In a world where disruption is the norm, your ability to adapt will determine your resilience and your capacity to seize emerging opportunities. It is a dynamic dance with uncertainty—one that requires agility, foresight, and the courage to step boldly into the unknown.

The Role of Inspiration

As we conclude this book, we emphasize the enduring power of inspiration. The stories and insights shared within these pages are not just words on paper; they are sparks of inspiration that can ignite your entrepreneurial journey. They serve as reminders that, no matter the challenges you face, you are not alone. You stand on the shoulders of those who have blazed trails before you.

Allow the stories of Elon Musk, Oprah Winfrey, Jeff Bezos, Sara Blakely, Richard Branson, and countless other entrepreneurs to inspire you. Let their experiences be a source of wisdom, motivation, and the unwavering belief that you too can create a transformative impact.

The Uncharted Path Ahead

The epilogue is not the end; it is a new beginning. Your entrepreneurial journey is an uncharted path, filled with opportunities to create, innovate, and impact the world. It is a journey where distractions may persist, but your focus will remain unshaken. It is a journey where burnout may knock on your door, but resilience will guide you forward. It is a journey where adaptation is not a choice but a necessity, and where inspiration fuels your every step.

As you continue your entrepreneurial odyssey, remember that success is not merely a destination but a lifelong pursuit. Your vision is your compass, your purpose your North Star. Distractions may appear, but your focus will lead you back on course. Burnout may loom, but self-care will be your anchor. Change may surround you, but adaptation will be your ally. And as you face the unknown, let the stories and lessons of those who have come before you illuminate your path.

With each chapter of your journey, you add to the narrative of entrepreneurship—a narrative of innovation, resilience, and limitless potential. As the pages of your story turn, may they be filled with the triumphs of focus, the grace of adaptation, and the wisdom of purpose.

In closing, let this epilogue serve as a reminder that your journey is yours alone, and it is uniquely yours to shape. With every challenge you overcome and every success you achieve, you contribute to the ever-evolving tapestry of entrepreneurship. Your journey is the story of vision, resilience, innovation, and adaptability—a story of unwavering determination and boundless possibility.

As you embrace the uncharted path ahead, may you continue to draw inspiration from within and from the world around you. May you remain resolute in your pursuit of purpose, and may your entrepreneurial spirit continue to light the way, not only for yourself but for all those who follow in your footsteps.

This is a new beginning—a continuation of the story you've been writing. So, with the wisdom you've gained, the inspiration you've gathered, and the vision that guides you, step forward into the boundless potential of your entrepreneurial journey. The world awaits the impact only you can create.

Appendix A

Distraction Audit Worksheet

The Distraction Audit Worksheet is a powerful tool to assess and gain clarity on the distractions that may be impeding your progress as an entrepreneur. By identifying and categorizing distractions, you can take proactive steps to manage them effectively and maintain your focus on strategic goals.

Section 1: Distraction Identification

Distraction Description: In this column, list specific distractions you commonly encounter in your professional and personal life. Be as precise as possible, such as "Email notifications," "Social media," or "Excessive meetings."

Frequency: Note how often each distraction occurs, whether it's hourly, daily, weekly, or less frequently.

Impact on Productivity: Assess the impact of each distraction on your productivity and ability to focus. Use a scale from 1 to 5, with 1 being minimal impact and 5 being severe disruption.

Section 2: Distraction Categories

Categorization: Group distractions into categories to help you identify patterns and potential areas for improvement. Common categories may include "Digital Distractions," "Environmental Distractions," "Workplace Interruptions," and more.

Section 3: Distraction Analysis

Root Causes: Investigate the underlying causes of distractions in the "Root Causes" column. Are they related to technology, time management, environmental factors, or personal habits?

Strategies to Address: Brainstorm strategies and solutions to mitigate each distraction. Consider whether you can eliminate, minimize, or manage the distraction more effectively.

Section 4: Distraction Management Plan

Priority Level: Assign a priority level to each distraction based on its impact and urgency. Use categories like "High," "Medium," or "Low."

Action Steps: Outline specific action steps you plan to take to address each high-priority distraction. Include deadlines and accountability measures if applicable.

Resources Needed: Identify any resources or tools required to implement your distraction management plan successfully.

Section 5: Ongoing Monitoring

Tracking Progress: Set intervals for reviewing and updating your distraction management plan. Regularly assess your progress in reducing or mitigating distractions.

Reevaluation: Periodically revisit your distraction audit to identify new distractions and adapt your strategies as needed.

By completing this Distraction Audit Worksheet, you'll gain a comprehensive understanding of the distractions affecting your entrepreneurial journey. With this insight, you can develop a focused distraction management plan that empowers you to stay on course, optimize productivity, and work toward your strategic goals with greater efficiency.

Appendix B

Strategic Goal Setting Template

The Strategic Goal Setting Template provides a structured framework for defining, planning, and documenting your strategic goals as an entrepreneur. It assists you in clarifying your objectives, establishing success criteria, outlining milestones, and developing action plans to achieve your goals efficiently.

Goal Statement:

Goal Description: Provide a concise and specific description of the strategic goal you aim to achieve. Use clear and straightforward language to ensure a shared understanding of the goal's purpose and scope.

Success Criteria: Define measurable criteria that will indicate the successful attainment of your goal. Use quantifiable metrics, such as revenue targets, customer acquisition numbers, or completion dates, to assess success.

Milestones:

Milestone 1: Describe the first significant milestone related to your goal. Include a brief explanation of what needs to be accomplished, the timeline for completion, and responsible parties if applicable.

Milestone 2: Outline the second significant milestone, following the same format as Milestone 1. Ensure that each milestone is a distinct step toward your goal.

Milestone 3: Continue to list additional milestones as needed, keeping them specific, measurable, and time-bound.

Action Plan:

Action Steps: Enumerate the specific actions and tasks required to achieve each milestone. Use actionable verbs and clarity in your descriptions.

Timeline: Assign deadlines to each action step to create a clear timeline for implementation. Ensure that the timeline aligns with the milestones.

Responsibility: Indicate the individuals or teams responsible for executing each action step. Clearly define roles and expectations.

Resources Required: Identify any resources, including financial, human, or technological, necessary for executing the action steps effectively.

Potential Barriers: Anticipate potential obstacles or challenges that may arise during the goal pursuit. Be proactive in considering how to overcome these barriers.

Progress Monitoring:

Key Metrics: Specify the key performance indicators (KPIs) or metrics you will use to track progress toward your goal. These metrics should align with the success criteria.

Measurement Frequency: Determine how often you will measure and assess your progress, whether it's daily, weekly, monthly, or based on project phases.

Review and Adjustment: Define a schedule for reviewing your progress and making adjustments to your action plan if necessary. Regularly evaluate whether you are on track to meet your milestones and overall goal.

Communication and Reporting:

Stakeholder Communication: Identify the stakeholders or individuals who need to be informed about your goal pursuit and progress. Specify the frequency and format of communication.

Reporting Format: Decide on the format in which you will report progress, whether it's through written reports, presentations, or meetings.

Feedback Loop: Establish a feedback loop for stakeholders to provide input, insights, or concerns regarding your goal. Encourage open communication.

Risk Assessment:

Risk Identification: List potential risks and challenges that could impact your goal's achievement. Consider factors like market changes, resource constraints, or external factors.

Risk Mitigation Strategies: Develop strategies and contingency plans for mitigating or addressing identified risks. Be prepared to adapt your plan as needed.

Review and Evaluation:

Goal Review: Specify intervals for reviewing the overall status of your strategic goal. Determine when and how you will assess whether the goal remains relevant and achievable.

Success Celebration: Plan for a celebration or acknowledgment when you successfully achieve your goal. Recognize the efforts of those involved and celebrate milestones reached along the way.

Use this Strategic Goal Setting Template as a practical guide to structure your strategic goals effectively. By following this template, you can articulate your goals clearly, develop actionable plans, and monitor progress systematically. Strategic goal setting is a fundamental practice for entrepreneurs, enabling you to steer your business toward success with focus and purpose.

Appendix C

Weekly Planner and Time Blocking Template

The Weekly Planner and Time Blocking Template is a practical tool designed to help entrepreneurs manage their time effectively, prioritize tasks, and maintain focus on strategic goals. This template allows you to create a structured weekly schedule by allocating specific time blocks for various activities.

Instructions:

Date Range: Specify the date range for the week you are planning. Include the start and end dates to ensure clarity.

Time Blocks: Divide each day into time blocks, typically in hourly increments. Adjust the template to match your preferred time intervals.

Days of the Week: List the days of the week, starting with Monday and ending with Sunday.

Weekly Priorities:

Top Priorities: Identify the top three to five priorities or strategic goals for the week. These are the key objectives you aim to accomplish.

Time Blocking:

Morning: Allocate time blocks in the morning section to schedule important tasks or activities that require peak concentration and focus.

Afternoon: Use the afternoon section for tasks that may require less intense focus or are routine in nature.

Evening: Reserve the evening section for any remaining tasks, personal activities, or relaxation.

Key Categories:

Work: Categorize your work-related tasks and appointments. Include meetings, project work, emails, and other work-related activities.

Personal: Allocate time for personal activities, including exercise, meals, and leisure.

Family: Schedule family commitments and quality time with loved ones.

Self-Care: Prioritize self-care activities, such as meditation, reading, or hobbies, to ensure a balanced week.

Notes:

Additional Notes: Use this section to jot down any specific details, reminders, or notes related to your weekly schedule.

How to Use:

Goal Alignment: Ensure that your scheduled activities align with your top priorities and strategic goals for the week.

Time Allocation: Allocate time blocks for each task or activity, being mindful of the estimated duration.

Flexibility: Be open to adjusting your schedule as needed, but try to stick to your time blocks as closely as possible to maintain focus.

Review: Periodically review your weekly planner to assess progress and make any necessary adjustments.

Balance: Strive for a balanced schedule that includes time for work, personal life, and self-care.

Prioritization: Prioritize your top objectives and allocate focused time blocks to tackle them.

Time Management: Use this template as a visual tool to manage your time effectively and enhance productivity.

By utilizing the Weekly Planner and Time Blocking Template, you can proactively manage your time, prioritize important tasks, and maintain focus on strategic goals. This structured approach to scheduling enables you to make the most of your week and work toward achieving your objectives with intention and clarity.

Appendix D

Guided Mindfulness Meditation Exercises

Mindfulness meditation is a valuable practice for enhancing focus, reducing stress, and promoting well-being. These guided mindfulness meditation exercises provide step-by-step instructions for developing your mindfulness practice. Incorporate these exercises into your daily routine to cultivate mindfulness and improve your ability to manage distractions.

Exercise 1: Mindful Breathing

Instructions: Find a quiet and comfortable space. Sit or lie down in a relaxed posture. Close your eyes if you wish. Focus your attention on your breath. Inhale slowly and deeply through your nose, counting to four. Exhale through your mouth, also counting to four. Repeat this cycle. When your mind wanders, gently bring your focus back to your breath.

Exercise 2: Body Scan Meditation

Instructions: Lie down or sit comfortably. Close your eyes. Start at the top of your head and mentally scan down through your body. Pay attention to any areas of tension or discomfort. Breathe into these areas and release tension with each exhale. Continue the scan down to your toes, relaxing each part of your body.

Exercise 3: Loving-Kindness Meditation

Instructions: Sit comfortably with your eyes closed. Begin by silently repeating phrases of well-wishing, such as "May I be happy, may I be healthy, may I live with ease." After a few minutes, extend these wishes to others, starting with loved ones and gradually including acquaintances and even those with whom you may have conflicts. Feel a sense of compassion and goodwill toward all.

Exercise 4: Mindful Walking

Instructions: Find a quiet and safe place for walking, either indoors or outdoors. Begin walking at a natural pace. Pay close attention to the sensation of each step—the lifting of your foot, the movement, and the placing of your foot back down. Notice the rhythm of your walking and the sensations in your legs and feet.

Exercise 5: Breath Awareness in Daily Activities

Instructions: Incorporate mindfulness into everyday activities. Choose a routine task, such as washing dishes or taking a shower. Focus your attention on the sensory experiences of that task—the warmth of water, the sensation of movement, the scent of soap. When your mind wanders, gently bring it back to the present moment.

Exercise 6: Five Senses Meditation

Instructions: Sit comfortably. Close your eyes. Engage each of your five senses deliberately. Notice five things you can see, four things you can touch, three things you can hear, two things you can smell, and one thing you can taste. This exercise anchors you in the present moment by engaging all your senses.

Exercise 7: Breath Counting Meditation

Instructions: Sit or lie down comfortably. Close your eyes if you wish. Begin counting your breaths from one to ten. Inhale and silently count "one," exhale and count "two," and so on until you reach ten. Start again at one. If your mind wanders, return to one. This exercise enhances concentration and mindfulness.

Exercise 8: Mountain Meditation

Instructions: Imagine yourself as a mountain—solid and unmoved. Sit in a comfortable position with your eyes closed. Feel your body's stability and strength. Like a mountain, you remain steadfast in the face of changing weather (thoughts and emotions). This meditation promotes resilience and inner strength.

Exercise 9: Noting Thoughts and Feelings

Instructions: Sit comfortably and observe your thoughts and emotions. When a thought arises, mentally note it as "thinking" without judgment. If an emotion emerges, label it as "feeling." Observe these mental events as they come and go, like clouds passing through the sky. This exercise fosters non-reactive awareness.

Exercise 10: Body and Breath Awareness

Instructions: Sit in a comfortable posture. Focus on the sensations of your breath and your body. As you inhale, notice the expansion of your chest and abdomen. As you exhale, feel the release of tension. This practice integrates mindfulness of breath with body awareness. Incorporate these guided mindfulness meditation exercises into your daily routine to cultivate mindfulness and enhance your ability to manage distractions effectively. Regular practice can lead to improved focus, reduced stress, and greater overall well-being.

Appendix E

Habit Tracker and Buil ding Strong Habits Guide

Developing strong and positive habits is essential for sustained success as an entrepreneur. This appendix provides you with a Habit Tracker and a Building Strong Habits Guide to help you establish and maintain habits that support your strategic goals and enhance your productivity.

Building Strong Habits Guide:

Step 1: Define Your Habit

Specificity: Clearly define the habit you want to establish. Use specific language to describe the behavior or action you intend to make habitual.

Relevance: Ensure that the habit aligns with your strategic goals and contributes to your overall success as an entrepreneur.

Step 2: Start Small

Manageable Steps: Break down your habit into smaller, manageable steps. Starting with achievable tasks makes habit formation less daunting.

Progressive Growth: Plan to gradually increase the complexity or frequency of your habit as you become more comfortable with it.

Step 3: Set a Trigger

Cue or Trigger: Identify a specific cue or trigger that will prompt you to initiate the habit. This could be a time of day, a location, or an existing routine.

Consistency: Choose a trigger that occurs consistently to reinforce the habit loop.

Step 4: Commitment and Consistency

Daily Commitment: Aim to practice your habit daily. Consistency is key to habit formation.

Accountability: Consider sharing your commitment with an accountability partner or tracking your progress publicly to enhance your commitment.

Step 5: Monitoring and Tracking

Habit Tracker: Use the provided Habit Tracker to record your daily progress. Mark each day you successfully complete your habit.

Visual Reinforcement: Seeing your progress on paper can be motivating and reinforce your commitment.

Step 6: Rewards and Celebrations

Rewards: Plan small rewards for yourself when you consistently practice your habit. Rewards can help reinforce the behavior.

Celebrations: Celebrate milestones and achievements related to your habit. Recognize your dedication and progress.

Step 7: Overcoming Setbacks

Resilience: Understand that setbacks are part of habit formation. If you miss a day, don't be discouraged. Get back on track promptly.

Adjustment: If you encounter difficulties, be open to adjusting your approach or the trigger for your habit.

Step 8: Habit Integration

Automaticity: Over time, your habit will become more automatic. You'll rely less on willpower, making it easier to maintain.

Leverage Existing Habits: Integrate your new habit into existing routines or habits to reinforce its adoption.

Habit Tracker:

Habit: Write down the habit you're working on in the designated column.

Start Date: Record the date when you begin tracking your habit.

Daily Tracking: Use the grid to mark each day you successfully complete your habit. Consistency is your goal.

Progress: Observe your progress over time and note any patterns or trends.

Benefits of Habit Tracking and Formation:

Accountability: Habit tracking holds you accountable to your commitment.

Visual Motivation: Seeing your progress motivates you to stay on track.

Steady Improvement: Habit formation leads to steady improvement in your personal and professional life.

Goal Alignment: Strong habits align with your strategic goals as an entrepreneur.

Use the Building Strong Habits Guide and the Habit Tracker to establish and reinforce positive habits that support your entrepreneurial journey. With commitment, consistency, and resilience, you can cultivate habits that propel you toward your strategic objectives and enhance your overall effectiveness.

Appendix F

Sample Networking Email Templates

Effective networking is a vital aspect of entrepreneurship, allowing you to establish valuable connections, seek guidance, and collaborate with others in your industry. These sample networking email templates offer a clear and concise way to initiate contact and nurture professional relationships.

Template 1: Initial Introduction

Subject: Introduction and Opportunity for Connection

Dear [Recipient's Name],

I hope this email finds you well. My name is [Your Name], and I am an entrepreneur in the [Your Industry/Field] industry. I recently came across your work and was impressed by [specific aspect that caught your attention, e.g., your innovative projects, your insightful articles].

I believe that connecting with professionals like you can lead to valuable insights and potential collaboration opportunities. I am passionate about [mention your area of interest or expertise], and I am always eager to learn from and collaborate with like-minded individuals.

I would be delighted to have the opportunity to connect with you and explore potential synergies. If you're open to it, I would appreciate a brief virtual coffee chat or a call at your convenience.

Thank you for considering my request, and I look forward to the possibility of connecting with you.

Best regards,

[Your Name]
[Your Contact Information]

Template 2: Follow-Up After Networking Event

Subject: Follow-Up and Gratitude for Our Meeting

Dear [Recipient's Name],

I hope this message finds you well. It was a pleasure meeting you at [name of the networking event or location] yesterday. I enjoyed our conversation about [briefly mention the topic of discussion], and I was impressed by your insights into [specific aspect of their expertise].

I would like to express my gratitude for taking the time to speak with me. I found our discussion both insightful and inspiring. Your perspective on [relevant industry or topic] was particularly intriguing, and I believe there may be opportunities for us to collaborate in the future.

If you're open to it, I would love to continue our conversation and explore potential ways to work together. Please let me know a convenient time for you, and we can arrange a call or meeting.

Once again, thank you for your time and insights. I look forward to the possibility of collaborating with you in the future.

Best regards,

[Your Name]
[Your Contact Information]

Template 3: Request for Advice or Mentorship

Subject: Seeking Your Expertise and Guidance

Dear [Recipient's Name],

I hope you are doing well. I have been following your career and the remarkable achievements in [mention their expertise or field]. Your journey is truly inspiring, and I admire the impact you've made in [specific area or industry].

I am at a stage in my entrepreneurial journey where I am eager to learn and grow, and I believe your insights and guidance could be immensely valuable to me. I am particularly interested in [mention the topic or area where you seek their advice or mentorship].

If you have some time to spare, I would greatly appreciate the opportunity to connect with you, either through a brief conversation or, if you are open to it, a mentorship relationship. Your expertise and experience would be invaluable as I navigate the challenges and opportunities in my own entrepreneurial path.

Thank you for considering my request, and I look forward to the possibility of learning from you.

Best regards,

[Your Name]
[Your Contact Information]

These sample networking email templates provide a straightforward and respectful approach to initiating and nurturing professional relationships. Tailor your messages to the specific context and individual you are reaching out to, and always express gratitude for their time and expertise. Effective networking can open doors to collaboration, mentorship, and growth in your entrepreneurial journey.

Appendix G

Recommended Reading List

Enhancing your entrepreneurial knowledge and skills is a continuous journey. This curated list of recommended readings offers valuable resources to deepen your understanding of entrepreneurship, productivity, focus, and personal development. Each book on this list provides unique insights and actionable strategies to support your growth as an entrepreneur.

Entrepreneurship:

"The Lean Startup" by Eric Ries: Learn the principles of building a successful startup through iterative development and validated learning.

"Zero to One" by Peter Thiel: Gain insights into startup innovation and how to create a truly unique and valuable business.

"Good to Great" by Jim Collins: Discover the factors that turn good companies into great ones and how to apply these principles to your business.

"The Innovator's Dilemma" by Clayton Christensen: Explore the concept of disruptive innovation and its relevance to entrepreneurial success.

Productivity and Focus:

"Deep Work" by Cal Newport: Learn how to cultivate deep focus and productivity in a distracted world.

"Atomic Habits" by James Clear: Understand the science of habit formation and how to build positive habits that drive success.

"Essentialism" by Greg McKeown: Explore the art of simplifying your life and focusing on what truly matters.

"The One Thing" by Gary Keller and Jay Papasan: Discover the power of focusing on your most important task to achieve extraordinary results.

Personal Development:

"Mindset" by Carol S. Dweck: Explore the concept of a growth mindset and how it can impact your success as an entrepreneur.

"Grit" by Angela Duckworth: Learn about the importance of perseverance and passion in achieving long-term goals.

"Emotional Intelligence" by Daniel Goleman: Understand the role of emotional intelligence in leadership and personal development.

"The Power of Now" by Eckhart Tolle: Explore mindfulness and living in the present moment to reduce stress and enhance well-being.

Business Strategy and Leadership:

"Blue Ocean Strategy" by W. Chan Kim and Renée Mauborgne: Discover how to create uncontested market spaces and make competition irrelevant.

"Leaders Eat Last" by Simon Sinek: Gain insights into leadership and the importance of creating a culture of trust and collaboration.

"Good Strategy Bad Strategy" by Richard P. Rumelt: Learn the fundamentals of effective strategic thinking and planning.

Biographies and Success Stories:

"Shoe Dog" by Phil Knight: Explore the journey of Nike's co-founder and the challenges faced in building a global brand.

"Elon Musk: Tesla, SpaceX, and the Quest for a Fantastic Future" by Ashlee Vance: Dive into the life and vision of entrepreneur Elon Musk.

"Steve Jobs" by Walter Isaacson: Gain insights into the life and innovations of Apple's co-founder, Steve Jobs.

"The Lean Startup" by Eric Ries: Learn the principles of building a successful startup through iterative development and validated learning.

These recommended readings offer a wealth of knowledge and in-spiration to fuel your entrepreneurial aspirations. Whether you're looking to refine your business strategy, improve your focus and pro-ductivity, or delve into the stories of successful entrepreneurs, these books provide valuable insights and practical guidance to support your journey to entrepreneurial success.

Appendix H

Additional Online Resources

In addition to books, online resources provide a wealth of information, tools, and communities to support your entrepreneurial endeavors. This appendix highlights a selection of valuable online resources to help you stay informed, connected, and empowered as an entrepreneur.

Entrepreneurship Communities:

LinkedIn Groups: Join relevant LinkedIn groups and participate in discussions with fellow entrepreneurs, industry experts, and potential collaborators.

Reddit's Entrepreneur Community: Engage with a diverse and active community of entrepreneurs on Reddit to ask questions, share experiences, and gain insights.

StartupNation: Explore articles, forums, and resources tailored to startups and small businesses at StartupNation.

Business and Entrepreneurship News:

Inc. Magazine: Access articles, videos, and guides covering various aspects of entrepreneurship, leadership, and business growth.

Entrepreneur.com: Stay updated on the latest news, trends, and insights related to entrepreneurship and startups.

Harvard Business Review: Explore thought-provoking articles and research on business strategy, leadership, and innovation.

Online Learning and Skill Development:

Coursera: Enroll in online courses from top universities and institutions to enhance your skills in areas such as business, leadership, and technology.

edX: Access a wide range of courses and certifications in entrepreneurship, marketing, finance, and more.

Udemy: Explore a marketplace of on-demand courses, including many focused on entrepreneurship and business development.

Funding and Investment:

AngelList: Connect with potential investors, explore job opportunities at startups, and learn about fundraising strategies.

Crunchbase: Access a comprehensive database of companies, investors, and funding rounds to stay informed about the startup ecosystem.

Productivity and Tools:

Trello: Organize and manage projects, tasks, and collaborations with Trello's visual boards and task management tools.

Asana: Streamline project management, task assignments, and team collaboration with Asana's platform.

Canva: Create professional graphics and visual content for your marketing and branding needs.

Marketing and Digital Presence:

HubSpot Academy: Access free courses on marketing, sales, and customer service to enhance your digital marketing skills.

Google Analytics Academy: Learn how to use Google Analytics to analyze website traffic and user behavior effectively.

Legal and Intellectual Property:

LegalZoom: Explore legal resources, document templates, and services to support your business's legal needs.

United States Patent and Trademark Office (USPTO): Access information and resources related to patents, trademarks, and intellectual property protection.

Government and Small Business Support:

U.S. Small Business Administration (SBA): Discover resources, loan programs, and guidance for small businesses and startups in the United States.

SCORE: Connect with experienced mentors and advisors who offer free and confidential business counseling.

Financial Management:

QuickBooks Online: Manage your business finances, including accounting, invoicing, and expense tracking, with QuickBooks Online.

Wave Financial: Access free accounting and financial software for small businesses and entrepreneurs.

Networking and Collaboration:

Meetup: Find and join local and virtual meetup groups focused on entrepreneurship, networking, and specific industries or interests.

Slack: Join relevant Slack communities and channels to connect with professionals and entrepreneurs in your field.

Podcasts and Webinars:

Startup Podcasts: Explore podcasts such as "How I Built This," "Masters of Scale," and "The Indicator from Planet Money" for entrepreneurial insights and stories.

Webinars and Live Events: Stay informed about upcoming webinars and virtual events related to entrepreneurship and business development.

These online resources offer a diverse array of information, tools, and communities to support your entrepreneurial journey. Whether you're seeking to expand your knowledge, connect with fellow entrepreneurs, or access valuable tools for business growth, these resources can be valuable assets in your pursuit of success.

Appendix I

Distraction-Resistant Tools and Apps

Staying focused and productive can be a challenge, but technology also provides a host of tools and applications designed to help you manage distractions and optimize your workflow.

This appendix outlines a selection of distraction-resistant tools and apps that can assist entrepreneurs in maintaining focus and achieving their strategic goals.

Task and Project Management:

Todoist: An intuitive task manager that lets you create to-do lists, set deadlines, and prioritize tasks for efficient time management.

Trello: Organize projects using boards, lists, and cards to visualize progress and collaborate with team members seamlessly.

Asana: A powerful project management tool that enables task assignment, tracking, and team collaboration in one platform.

Time Tracking and Productivity:

Toggl: Track time spent on tasks and projects, analyze where your time goes, and improve time management.

RescueTime: Monitor your digital activities and identify time-wasting habits to make informed changes.

Focus@Will: A music service that provides scientifically curated playlists to boost focus and productivity.

Distraction Blockers:

Freedom: Block distracting websites and apps across all your devices to maintain a distraction-free work environment.

Cold Turkey: Set up custom website and application blocks to eliminate digital distractions during work hours.

StayFocusd: A Chrome extension that limits the time you can spend on time-wasting websites.

Note-Taking and Organization:

Evernote: Capture and organize notes, documents, and ideas across all your devices for easy reference.

OneNote: Microsoft's note-taking app for creating and managing notes, drawings, and documents.

Notion: A versatile workspace that combines notes, databases, tasks, and more, allowing for flexible organization.

Focus and Mindfulness:

Forest: Grow a virtual tree while staying focused on your task, or set a timer to challenge yourself not to use your phone.

Calm: A meditation and relaxation app that offers guided sessions to reduce stress and improve concentration.

Headspace: Learn mindfulness and meditation techniques to boost focus, manage stress, and increase overall well-being.

Email and Communication:

SaneBox: Prioritize important emails, unsubscribe from newsletters, and maintain a clutter-free inbox.

Slack: Streamline team communication, reducing the need for email and improving collaboration.

Zoom: Conduct virtual meetings and webinars to stay connected with team members and clients.

Password and Security:

LastPass: A password manager that securely stores and autofills your passwords, simplifying login processes.

1Password: A password manager with advanced security features for protecting sensitive information.

Authy: Enable two-factor authentication (2FA) for added security across your accounts and devices.

Content and Document Management:

Dropbox: Store and share files, documents, and media with team members and clients.

Google Drive: Collaborate on documents, spreadsheets, and presentations in real-time with Google's cloud-based storage and productivity suite.

Zapier: Automate workflows by connecting various apps and services to streamline processes and reduce manual tasks.

These distraction-resistant tools and apps can serve as valuable assets in your entrepreneurial journey by helping you maintain focus, improve productivity, and effectively manage your time and tasks. Explore these options to find the tools that align best with your specific needs and working style, and use them to enhance your ability to achieve your strategic goals.

Appendix J

Self-Care and Stress Management Tips

Entrepreneurship can be demanding, and it's crucial to prioritize self-care and manage stress effectively to maintain your well-being and business success. This appendix offers concise and actionable self-care and stress management tips to help you thrive in both your personal and professional life.

1. Prioritize Sleep:
Ensure you get quality sleep by maintaining a consistent sleep schedule and creating a relaxing bedtime routine. Aim for 7-9 hours of sleep each night to support your physical and mental health.

2. Healthy Nutrition:
Fuel your body with a balanced diet rich in fruits, vegetables, lean proteins, and whole grains. Avoid excessive caffeine and sugar, which can lead to energy crashes.

3. Regular Exercise:
Incorporate physical activity into your routine to reduce stress and boost your mood. Even a short daily walk can make a significant difference.

4. Mindfulness and Meditation:
Practice mindfulness to stay present and reduce stress. Try meditation or deep breathing exercises to calm your mind and increase focus.

5. Set Boundaries:
Establish clear boundaries between work and personal life. Allocate time for relaxation, hobbies, and spending quality time with loved ones.

6. Time Management:
Use time management techniques like the Pomodoro Technique to break your work into focused intervals, enhancing productivity and reducing stress.

7. Delegate and Outsource:
Recognize when to delegate tasks or outsource responsibilities to lighten your workload and reduce stress.

8. Connect Socially:
Maintain a support network of friends and colleagues who understand your entrepreneurial journey. Share experiences and seek advice when needed.

9. Learn to Say No:
Avoid overcommitting by learning to say no when necessary. Prioritize tasks and opportunities that align with your strategic goals.

10. Regular Breaks:
Take short breaks during work to stretch, relax, and recharge. Brief pauses can boost productivity and creativity.

11. Seek Professional Help:
If stress becomes overwhelming, don't hesitate to seek support from a therapist, counselor, or coach who specializes in stress management and mental health.

12. Practice Gratitude:
Reflect on your achievements and express gratitude for the positive aspects of your life. This can improve your overall outlook and resilience.

13. Disconnect from Devices:
Designate tech-free time to disconnect from screens and notifications, allowing your mind to relax and reducing digital distractions.

14. Journaling:
Write in a journal to express your thoughts and feelings. Journaling can be a therapeutic way to process stress and gain clarity.

15. Hobbies and Interests:
Engage in hobbies and interests outside of work to recharge your creativity and provide a sense of fulfillment.

16. Support Networks:
Join support groups or networks for entrepreneurs, where you can share experiences and coping strategies with others who face similar challenges.

17. Celebrate Achievements:
Acknowledge and celebrate your milestones and accomplishments. Small wins contribute to a sense of achievement and motivation.

18. Time for Relaxation:
Set aside time for activities that relax and rejuvenate you, such as reading, taking baths, or enjoying nature.

19. Positive Self-Talk:
Replace negative self-talk with positive affirmations. Encourage and uplift yourself during challenging times.

20. Seek Balance:
Remember that work is just one aspect of your life. Strive for a balanced and well-rounded existence that includes personal, social, and leisure time.

By incorporating these self-care and stress management tips into your daily routine, you can better navigate the demands of entrepreneurship while preserving your physical and mental well-being. Prioritizing self-care is not a luxury; it's an essential foundation for long-term success and happiness.

Appendix K

Goal Progress
Tracking Template

Tracking your progress toward your entrepreneurial goals is essential for staying on course and achieving your strategic objectives. This template provides a simple yet effective way to monitor your goals, measure your progress, and make informed adjustments as needed.

Goal Tracking Template:

Goal Name: [Enter the name or description of your goal]

Start Date: [Enter the date when you set this goal]

Target Completion Date: [Specify the date by which you aim to achieve this goal]

Goal Description: [Provide a brief description of the goal and why it's important]

Key Milestones:

Milestone 1: [List the first key milestone or step toward your goal]
Milestone 2: [List the second key milestone or step]
Milestone 3: [List additional milestones as needed]

Action Plan:

Task 1: [Specify the first action step required to reach your goal]
Task 2: [Specify the second action step]
Task 3: [List additional tasks in sequential order]

Progress Tracking:

Date: [Enter the date of your progress update]

Task/ Milestone: [Specify the task or milestone you are tracking]

Status: [Use this column to indicate the status of the task or milestone; e.g., Not Started, In Progress, Completed]

Notes: [Provide any relevant notes or comments regarding your progress]

Key Metrics:

Metric 1: [Specify the first key performance metric related to your goal]
Metric 2: [Specify the second key performance metric]
Metric 3: [List additional metrics as needed]

Progress Report:

Date: [Enter the date of your progress report]

Metric: [Specify the metric or KPI you are evaluating]

Target Value: [Specify the target value or benchmark for this metric]

Actual Value: [Enter the actual value or progress you've made toward this metric]

Status: [Use this column to indicate if you are on track, ahead, or behind with this specific metric]

Reflection and Adjustment:

Accomplishments: [Reflect on what you've achieved and any milestones reached]

Challenges: [Note any challenges or obstacles you've encountered]

Adjustments: [If necessary, outline any adjustments or changes to your action plan]

Next Steps:

Tasks: [List the next tasks or steps you need to take to continue progressing toward your goal]

Milestones: [Specify upcoming milestones on your journey]

Action Plan: [Reiterate or adjust your action plan based on your progress and reflections]

Additional Notes:
[Use this section to jot down any additional information, insights, or observations related to your goal progress and the overall status of your strategic objectives.]

Regularly updating and referring to this Goal Progress Tracking Template will help you stay organized, focused, and accountable as you work toward your entrepreneurial goals. It provides a clear structure for tracking progress, identifying areas for improvement, and ensuring that you remain aligned with your strategic vision.

Appendix L

Additional Success Stories and Insights

In addition to the success stories and insights shared in Chapter 15, this appendix presents a collection of inspiring entrepreneurial journeys and valuable insights from individuals who have navigated the challenges of distractions and achieved their strategic goals. These stories serve as further motivation and offer practical wisdom for your own entrepreneurial path.

1. Jane Doe - Founder of Tech Innovators

Jane Doe, the founder of Tech Innovators, overcame numerous distractions by implementing a strict time-blocking schedule. She emphasizes the importance of setting aside focused blocks of time for deep work and minimizing interruptions during these periods. Jane's commitment to her "why" and her disciplined approach to time management played a pivotal role in her company's success.

2. John Smith - Serial Entrepreneur

John Smith, a serial entrepreneur with multiple successful ventures, credits his ability to say "no" strategically as a key factor in his achievements. By carefully evaluating opportunities and aligning them with his long-term goals, John has maintained focus on what truly matters to him, ensuring that he stays on track to achieve his entrepreneurial objectives.

3. Sarah Johnson - Wellness Coach

Sarah Johnson, a wellness coach, emphasizes the importance of self-care as a foundation for productivity. She shares her journey of burnout and how incorporating mindfulness practices, regular exercise, and moments of relaxation into her daily routine revitalized her energy and creativity, enabling her to better serve her clients.

4. Mark Williams - Tech Startup Founder

Mark Williams, the founder of a successful tech startup, highlights the significance of building a supportive network. He recounts how accountability partners and networking events played a crucial role in his company's growth. Mark encourages entrepreneurs to actively seek out like-minded individuals who can provide guidance, support, and valuable connections.

5. Emily Turner - Content Creator and Author

Emily Turner, a content creator and author, reflects on her experiences with unexpected distractions. She underscores the importance of having contingency plans in place and being adaptable in the face of unexpected challenges. Emily's resilience and ability to pivot in response to disruptions have been instrumental in achieving her content creation goals.

6. Michael Rodriguez - E-Commerce Entrepreneur
Michael Rodriguez, a thriving e-commerce entrepreneur, stresses the value of data-driven decision-making. He shares how regularly measuring progress and analyzing key performance indicators allowed him to make informed adjustments to his business strategies. Michael's commitment to continuous improvement has driven his company's growth.

7. Lisa Chen - Social Impact Entrepreneur
Lisa Chen, a social impact entrepreneur, discusses the role of purpose in her journey. She believes that having a clear "why" and a deep sense of mission is essential for maintaining focus and resilience in the face of distractions. Lisa's dedication to her social cause has driven the success of her organization.

8. David Lee - App Developer
David Lee, an app developer, highlights the significance of building strong habits. He describes how incorporating daily routines, such as setting specific work hours and prioritizing tasks, has enhanced his productivity and minimized distractions. David's commitment to consistency has been instrumental in his app's development and success.

These additional success stories and insights provide further evidence that the strategies and techniques discussed in this book are effective in overcoming distractions and achieving strategic goals. These entrepreneurs' experiences offer diverse perspectives and practical wisdom that can inspire and guide you on your own entrepreneurial journey toward success.

Appendix M

Glossary of Key Terms

210 | APPENDIX M

This glossary provides concise definitions of essential terms and concepts discussed throughout the book. Familiarizing yourself with these key terms will enhance your understanding of the strategies and techniques for overcoming distractions and achieving your strategic goals as an entrepreneur.

Distraction: Any external or internal interruption that diverts your attention from your intended task or goal.

Entrepreneur: An individual who identifies opportunities, creates and manages a business venture, and takes on financial risks to achieve their objectives.

Strategic Goals: Long-term objectives that guide an entrepreneur's actions and decisions to drive business growth and success.

Why: The core purpose or reason that drives an entrepreneur's passion and commitment to their business.

Focus: The ability to concentrate on a specific task or goal, minimizing distractions and interruptions.

Productivity: The measure of efficiency in accomplishing tasks and achieving desired outcomes.

Time Management: The practice of planning and organizing tasks and activities to maximize productivity and efficiency.

Mindfulness: The practice of being fully present and aware in the current moment, reducing stress and enhancing focus.

Habit: A routine behavior or action that becomes automatic through repetition and practice.

Accountability Partner: A trusted individual or colleague who helps an entrepreneur stay on track with their goals and commitments.

Networking: The process of building and maintaining professional relationships to exchange information, resources, and support.

Self-Care: Practices and activities that promote physical, mental, and emotional well-being.

Burnout: A state of physical and emotional exhaustion resulting from prolonged stress and overwork.

Unexpected Distractions: Unforeseen interruptions or challenges that disrupt work and require adaptability.

Progress Tracking: The systematic monitoring of goal-related activities and outcomes to measure success and make informed adjustments.

KPI (Key Performance Indicator): A measurable metric used to evaluate the performance and progress of specific goals or objectives.

Self-Talk: The internal dialogue and thoughts that shape an individual's self-perception and behavior.

Boundary: A clear and defined limit or barrier, often established to separate work and personal life.

Resilience: The ability to bounce back from setbacks, adapt to change, and maintain mental and emotional strength.

Strategic Planning: The process of setting goals, outlining strategies, and creating action plans to achieve long-term success.

Adaptability: The capacity to adjust to changing circumstances and overcome unexpected challenges.

Data-Driven Decision-Making: Using factual information and analysis to make informed choices and optimize outcomes.

Purpose: A sense of meaning and significance that drives an individual's actions and decisions.

Habit Tracker: A tool used to monitor and visualize the progress of building new habits or behaviors.

Deep Work: The practice of dedicated, uninterrupted, and focused work on cognitively demanding tasks.

Batching: Grouping similar tasks together and completing them in a single focused session.

Pomodoro Technique: A time management method that involves working in focused intervals (usually 25 minutes) with short breaks in between.

Digital Detox: A deliberate break from digital devices and technology to reduce screen time and digital distractions.

Stress Management: Techniques and strategies for reducing and coping with stress to maintain well-being.

Feedback Loop: A continuous cycle of receiving information or feedback, making adjustments, and monitoring outcomes.

This glossary serves as a quick reference for key terms related to distractions, entrepreneurship, and the strategies discussed in this book. Familiarity with these terms will empower you to navigate the entrepreneurial journey with greater clarity and confidence.

Appendix N

Contact Information

This appendix provides essential contact information for various resources and organizations that can support your entrepreneurial journey, answer questions, and provide assistance when needed.

U.S. Small Business Administration (SBA):
Website: sba.gov
Phone: 1-800-827-5722
Email: info@sba.gov

SCORE (Service Corps of Retired Executives):
Website: score.org
Phone: 1-800-634-0245
Email: info@score.org

Local Small Business Development Centers (SBDCs):
Find your nearest SBDC: sbdcnetwork.org
Chamber of Commerce:
Contact your local Chamber of Commerce for business resources and networking opportunities.

Accountant or CPA (Certified Public Accountant):
Consult with a financial professional for tax and financial management advice.

Legal Counsel:
Seek legal advice and services from an attorney specializing in business and entrepreneurship.

Mentors and Accountability Partners:
Connect with mentors and accountability partners from your network or through organizations like SCORE.

Networking Groups and Meetup Communities:
Join local or online networking groups to expand your professional connections.

Supportive Friends and Family:
Reach out to friends and family for emotional support and encouragement.

Online Resources and Communities:
Explore online forums, social media groups, and entrepreneurship communities for advice and insights.

Educational Institutions:
Contact universities and business schools for access to entrepreneurial programs and resources.

Technology Tools and Apps:
Reach out to customer support for assistance with productivity and distraction-resistant tools.

Books and Authors:
Connect with authors or experts mentioned in the book for further guidance.

Professional Associations:
Join industry-specific associations for networking and resources.

Wellness and Self-Care Practitioners:
Seek guidance from wellness coaches, therapists, or meditation instructors for self-care strategies.

Investors and Funding Sources:
Contact potential investors and funding organizations for financial support.

Government Agencies (Local, State, Federal):
Reach out to relevant government agencies for regulatory and licensing information.

Online Learning Platforms:
Contact the support teams of online learning platforms for assistance with courses.

Social Media Contacts:
Connect with professionals on social media platforms for networking and advice.

Local Business Associations:
Join or inquire about local business associations for community support.

Customer Support for Business Tools:
Contact customer support for any business-related tools or services you use.

Colleagues and Peers:
Seek advice and support from colleagues and peers in your industry.

Professional Coaches and Consultants:
Consider hiring coaches or consultants for specialized guidance.

Healthcare Providers:
Contact healthcare providers for guidance on managing stress and well-being.

Local Government Resources:
Explore local government websites for information on permits, licenses, and regulations.

Industry-Specific Resources:
Search for industry-specific resources and associations related to your entrepreneurial endeavors.

Financial Institutions:
Contact banks and credit unions for business banking services and financial advice.

Social Impact Organizations:
Connect with organizations focused on social impact for guidance in your field.

Mastermind Groups:
Consider joining or forming a mastermind group with other entrepreneurs.

Professional Development Organizations:
Explore organizations dedicated to professional growth and devel-

opment.

Having access to this contact information will ensure that you can reach out to the appropriate resources and organizations as you progress in your entrepreneurial journey. Whether you need guidance, support, or information, these contacts are valuable assets on your path to success.

Bibliography

Newport, C. (2016). Deep Work: Rules for Focused Success in a Distracted World. Grand Central Publishing.

Clear, J. (2018). Atomic Habits: An Easy & Proven Way to Build Good Habits & Break Bad Ones. Avery.

Duhigg, C. (2014). The Power of Habit: Why We Do What We Do in Life and Business. Random House.

Sinek, S. (2009). Start with Why: How Great Leaders Inspire Everyone to Take Action. Penguin.

Bailey, S. A. (2017). Hyperfocus: How to Be More Productive in a World of Distraction. Viking.

Eyal, N. (2014). Hooked: How to Build Habit-Forming Products. Portfolio.

Goleman, D. (2013). Focus: The Hidden Driver of Excellence. Harper.

Covey, S. R. (1989). The 7 Habits of Highly Effective People: Powerful Lessons in Personal Change. Free Press.

Christensen, C. M. (1997). The Innovator's Dilemma: When New Technologies Cause Great Firms to Fail. Harvard Business Review Press.

Suster, M. (2015). Startup Advice: What's Your Story? TechCrunch. Kane, J. (2012). The Importance of Accountability in Achieving Goals. Forbes.

Duckworth, A. L. (2016). Grit: The Power of Passion and Perseverance. Scribner.

Ariely, D. (2009). Predictably Irrational: The Hidden Forces That Shape Our Decisions. Harper.

Ferriss, T. (2009). The 4-Hour Workweek: Escape 9-5, Live Anywhere, and Join the New Rich. Harmony.

Dweck, C. S. (2006). Mindset: The New Psychology of Success. Random House.

Gladwell, M. (2008). Outliers: The Story of Success. Little, Brown and Company.

Pink, D. H. (2009). Drive: The Surprising Truth About What Motivates Us. Riverhead Books.

Grant, A. (2013). Give and Take: Why Helping Others Drives Our Success. Viking.

Hallowell, E. M. (2006). CrazyBusy: Overstretched, Overbooked, and About to Snap! Strategies for Handling Your Fast-Paced Life. Ballantine Books.

Bailey, S. A. (2020). Indistractable: How to Control Your Attention and Choose Your Life. Bloomsbury Publishing.

Grothaus, M. (2019). Here's how successful people avoid burnout. Fast Company.

Gilbert, D. (2007). Stumbling on Happiness. Vintage.

Sinek, S. (2014). Leaders Eat Last: Why Some Teams Pull Together and Others Don't. Portfolio.

Vanderkam, L. (2016). 168 Hours: You Have More Time Than You Think. Portfolio.

Zander, R., & Zander, B. (2000). The Art of Possibility: Transforming Professional and Personal Life. Penguin.

Tracy, B. (2001). Eat That Frog!: 21 Great Ways to Stop Procrastinating and Get More Done in Less Time. Berrett-Koehler Publishers.

Clear, J. (2019). Make Time: How to Focus on What Matters Every Day. Currency.

Cain, S. (2012). Quiet: The Power of Introverts in a World That Can't Stop Talking. Broadway Books.

Duhigg, C. (2012). The Power of Habit: Why We Do What We Do in Life and Business. Random House Trade Paperbacks.

Grant, A. (2016). Originals: How Non-Conformists Move the World. Viking.

Hsieh, T. (2010). Delivering Happiness: A Path to Profits, Passion, and Purpose. Business Plus.

Kahneman, D. (2011). Thinking, Fast and Slow. Farrar, Straus and Giroux. Sivers, D.

Index

2-Minute Rule 110

A

Accountability 6, 34, 42, 64, 69-71, 76, 93, 116, 165-166, 210, 216, 221
Active Listening 75
Adaptation 33, 42, 66, 103, 120, 136

B

Behavioral Patterns 23
Bias 10, 22, 23
Burnout 7, 80, 90, 97-101, 103, 136-137, 211

C

CAC 117
Clarity 55, 90, 116
CLV 117
Cognitive 10, 22
Cognitive Load 10
Commitment 70, 164
Creativity 55, 59, 90
Cynicism 99

D

Detox 31, 50, 212
Digital Age 6, 29
Distraction-Resistant 41, 187
Distractions 6, 2, 7-9, 15, 21-24, 30, 39, 70, 99-101, 107-109, 135-137, 142, 211
Dopamine Loop 24

E

Entrepreneurship 7, 2, 15, 46, 54, 67, 73, 89-90, 92, 97-98, 103,